In Our Lives First

MEDITATIONS FOR COUNSELORS

Diane Mandt Langberg, PhD

Diane Langberg PhD & Associates
JENKINTOWN, PENNSYLVANIA

Diane Langberg PhD & Associates
512 West Avenue
Jenkintown, PA 19046
www.dianelangberg.com
info@dianelangberg.com

Book Layout ©2013 BookDesignTemplates.com

Ordering Information:
Quantity sales. Special discounts are available on quantity purchases by corporations, associations, and others. For details, contact the "Special Sales Department" at the physical or email addresses above.

In Our Lives First/Diane Langberg. —1st ed.
ISBN 978-1-4974440-1-0

Contents

Week 3

Week 4

Week 5

Week 6

Dedication

To those in that great cloud of witnesses who have fed my soul and shown me Jesus

Foreward

As caregivers—psychologists, psychiatrists, counselors, pastors and lay helpers—the majority of us chose the work we do with those who suffer because it was in our hearts to do so and we believed we were called and gifted by God. We wanted to help and be a healing force. In following that call we have often landed in some hard and ugly places; places full of evil and darkness, deception and the exploitation of others. There is a cost in doing this work.

These short meditations are about understanding the work we do and its impact on our lives and souls. I have learned through the decades that our true work is actually not care giving or counseling but rather tending to our souls in relationship to Christ. We are handling toxic things; we have toxins in our own hearts and it is not hard to either be destroyed by the work or to destroy those who come to us for help. If we are to bring the life and love of Jesus Christ into flesh and blood realities then we must learn, as Oswald Chambers teaches, to "never allow anything to come between ourselves and Jesus Christ, no emotion, or experience; nothing must keep us from the one great sovereign source."[1] I pray these meditations born from a lifetime in the counselor's chair bless you and challenge your heart and mind to greater love and obedience to Christ.

---

[1] Oswald Chambers, *My Utmost for His Highest* in *The Complete Works of Oswald Chambers* (Grand Rapids, MI: Discovery House Publishers, 2000), p. 820, September 6. Used by permission; see References.

The meditations are grouped into six weeks' worth of readings, along with relevant quotations for you to ponder on the weekends. Weeks 1 and 2 focus on the primacy of our relationship with Jesus Christ and the necessity of cultivating in our own lives the growth we long to see in our clients—we cannot lead them where we have not gone first. Weeks 3 and 4 explore how these truths impact various aspects of the therapeutic process, while weeks 5 and 6 look to broader concerns within the church and the world. Feel free to read the essays in the order that most interests you, however. Accompanying each essay is a question for further reflection and a related quote or verse. I recommend that as you read each essay, you find one "take away" point to carry with you throughout the day, perhaps even writing it on a note card. The quotations have been gleaned from my favorite authors, most of them Puritan pastors and theologians who had profound insights into caring for souls—both their own and others.

These essays were first published in Christian Counseling Today in the column "An Inward Look," from 2000–2010, and were compiled, adapted, and edited by Dana Ergenbright and Philip Monroe. For bibliographic information about the essays, please see the References section at the end of the book.

Week 1

Counseling: A Dangerous Profession?

I wonder how many of us who are involved in counseling think of ourselves as engaging in a dangerous profession. After all, I am sitting in a nice chair, inside a nice office, talking to people. How could that be dangerous?

There are an interesting couple of verses in Ecclesiastes 10: "Whoever digs a pit may fall into it; whoever breaks through a wall may be bitten by a snake. Whoever quarries stones may be injured by them; whoever splits logs may be endangered by them" (vv. 8-9).

These words seem to suggest that there are dangers connected with our work and our lives of which it would be well for us to be aware. If whoever quarries stones may be injured by them, then what of the person who quarries sin and sorrow? If pits, walls, stones, and logs are dangerous, then how much more dangerous are abuse, addiction, rage, fear, and grief?

What sorts of dangers am I talking about? Have you ever heard someone's story and wondered whether or not God is good? Or maybe you have even wondered if He *is*? When we sit with lives broken by others—lives full of abuse, victimization, oppression, and injustice—who of us has not questioned the goodness, the faithfulness, or the wisdom of God?

Danger: Slander

I believe one of the dangers inherent in our quarrying is that it can lead us to slander the character of God. We begin to define Him according to the things we hear from others, rather than according to the things we hear from Him. We begin to see God through the lens of sin and sorrow, rather than viewing sin and sorrow through the lens of His character.

Danger: Erosion of Faith

Not only can our work lead us to slander God, it easily can also lead to an erosion of faith. The great majority of us who enter the profession of counseling do so optimistically. We believe that help exists, that there is hope of change, and that we can help bring those things about in the lives of others. We encounter difficult cases, maybe even cases others have given up on, and believe we can make the difference. We ride emotional roller coasters, pull others back from the brink of suicide, go one more round of rehab, and begin to doubt that change will come. And sometimes, in some lives change does not come. Our faith wavers. Where is this God who redeems? Why has this person not seen or heard God and been changed? Perhaps even more devastating to faith are those who refuse all help and defiantly continue lying, seducing, or abusing others. Ravaging wolves are loose in the church, destroying others, seemingly untouched and unrestrained. Where is God? As Amy Carmichael says, "Oh, there are things done in the world today would root up faith, but for Gethsemane."[2] One of the dangers of the work we do is its capacity to root up faith.

Danger: Self-righteousness

A final danger inherent in the work we do is the fact that sin is contagious. Spend five minutes with a group of critical people, and you will prove my point. Those who work with infectious diseases must keep in mind the fact that they can catch the disease they are trying to cure or ease if they are not careful. This principle is not limited to the physical realm. The roots of those sins we find abhorrent in others lie within us as well. If we are not aware of this, then we have fallen into deception and foolishness. And if we do not catch the disease with which we are working, then how supremely easy to become infected with pride and self-righteousness instead!

Let us not fool ourselves and think that functioning in a professional sphere with certain degrees protects us from danger. It is when we think ourselves safe that we are, in fact, in the greatest danger. May we stay vigilant, "dwelling in the shelter of the Most High...for it is he who delivers you from the snare of the evil one, and from the deadly disease" (Ps. 91:1-3, paraphrase).

---

[2] Amy Carmichael, *Rose from Brier* (Fort Washington, PA: CLC Publications, 2012), p. 192, "Calvary's Elucidation." Used by permission; see References.

For further thought:

What specific dangers to your soul are present in your work today?
What will you do to protect yourself from these dangers?

———————————

"Who can bear the weight of souls without sometimes sinking into the dust?"

C. H. Spurgeon[3]

———————————

[3] Charles Haddon Spurgeon, *Lectures to My Students: A Selection from Addresses Delivered to the Students of the Pastor's College, Metropolitan Tabernacle* (London: Passmore and Alabaster, 1875), p. 170, vol. 1, Lecture 11, "The Minister's Fainting Fits."

Finding Encouragement in Discouraging Work

I have encountered quite a few people in ministry and in counseling recently who seem very weary and discouraged. Both the needs and the brokenness of people seem overwhelming and the burden has grown very heavy for them.

Such weariness is not an uncommon experience, is it? We are told in 2 Chronicles 35:2 that Josiah, one of the good kings of Judah, "set the priests in their offices and encouraged them in the service of the house of the LORD" (NASB). Our God has set you in the office or ministry you have in the Body and would have you be encouraged today.

The word "encourage" literally means to put courage in. Courage comes from the Latin word "cor," meaning heart. When we encourage someone, we put heart back into him or her. When you are discouraged and weary it does feel like the heart has gone out of what you do, doesn't it? Things feel flat, insignificant, and overwhelming. Let me pass on to you some of the truths of God that have often been used to restore my soul, strengthen my heart, and renew my spirit.

Where are you looking for inspiration?

One of the things that happens to us in ministry of any kind is that the needs of people become our focus, our purpose. It is easy enough to get lost in the pain and suffering of those for whom we care. We have often been called to tend to those needs. We end up looking to those to whom we minister to provide us with meaning and motivation. We seek our inspiration from them.

God often has to remind me that He and He alone is the source of my inspiration, my courage. That which inspires me is behind me, under me, not in front of me. I am not to be dragged around by the needs of others. I am rather to be responding out of the deep well of God's love and in obedience to Him.

The Lord Jesus Christ Himself is my inspiration. When the dominant note of my life becomes what others need, I will drown. The needs of this world are far beyond my capacity to meet. I do not take my orders from the needs I see, but from my Lord.

How do you measure success?

Christ is not only the source for my work; He is also the outcome. If the dominant note is the needs of others, then success is measured by how many of those I meet. However, if Christ is to be the outcome of our work, then success becomes another thing altogether. Success, then, is what pleases Him, glorifies Him, and looks like Him. Success is not a body count of those who turned out a certain way. Success is rather whether or not I looked like Him no matter the outcome. We are in great danger when we put the emphasis on the results we see in the lives of others. The work of the Spirit in our lives is not evidenced in the number of people we fix, but in the character we manifest, whether people are fixed or not. What happens in the lives He brings across my path is under His jurisdiction, not mine.

The heart goes out of us when we are controlled by the needs of others and when we measure our success by their responses. Christ is the source of our work. Our service is in His house and for His sake. He is the goal of our work.

This God, who is both inspiration and goal, says to us when we are discouraged, "Come to me, all who are weary and heavy-laden, and I will give you rest. Take my yoke upon you, and learn of me, for I am gentle and humble in heart, and you will find rest for your souls. For my yoke is easy and my burden is light" (Matt. 11:28-30, NASB).

May you be encouraged today to find your inspiration, your goal, and your rest in Him.

For further thought:

Where in your work are you most discouraged or feel like a failure?
If Christ is the source and measure of success, how might this change your outlook?

"We consider what we do in the way of Christian work as service, yet Jesus Christ calls service to be what we are to Him, not what we do for Him."

Oswald Chambers[4]

---

[4] Oswald Chambers, *My Utmost for His Highest* in *The Complete Works of Oswald Chambers* (Grand Rapids, MI: Discovery House Publishers, 2000), p.792, June 19. Used by permission; see References. Also http://utmost.org/my-utmost-for-his-highest/

Prayer:
The Crux of Our Calling

When I talk with counselors, or listen to them talk among themselves about why they pursued counseling as an avenue of service, I often hear things such as: *"I wanted to help others," "I believe God has called me into this work,"* or *"I found healing through counseling and wanted to pass on what I was given."* Certainly these are true reasons. They are also good reasons.

Recently, however, I have been struck with the possibility of another reason why God may have called us into this vocation we call counseling—one I have never before heard expressed. Is it possible that God has called us into this work so that we might pray?

Think about it. You and I know things about people and situations that no one else knows. We know about marriages, abuse, violence, and sick churches. We know about things far beyond a particular counselee's specific life. Our counselees tell us about their histories, their church lives, their marital lives, and their communities. We hear information about individuals, churches, communities, organizations and even nations that we will never personally encounter or have direct influence over. I believe that God allows us to see and hear things so that we will help. That is without question.

We hear in order to pray

Is it not also possible that He brings us into contact with things in this world so that we will intercede? Our intercession can cover far more people and situations than we can ever help in the literal sense. It is as if God is saying, *"See this sin? Hear about My people? Comprehend this evil and its tentacles? Pray, child. Pray for all that I have put before you."*

It is in the process of interceding that God's purpose and wise order is brought about in this world.

When we pray, we are nourished

Prayer also nourishes the life of God in us. Prayer is not merely a way of getting things from God. Prayer is what enables us to know the mind of God regarding the matter for which we are praying. So much of what we work with is poisonous. We handle things like violence, torment, fear, abuse, deception, and despair. These things are toxic and have the potential to destroy us. We hear these things and think we know what to do and how to think about it. But do we?

How often do we set out to do the work, but then are surprised? It goes differently than we expected; it is harder than we thought. Counseling takes much longer than we dreamed possible, and it impacts in ways that catch us off guard. We get impatient, angry, afraid, hardened, cynical, and despairing.

Prayer is how we say to God, *"What is Your way? Why are my thoughts not like Yours? What work needs to be done in me? Why is my heart not reflective of Yours?"*

Prayer is the work of feeding God's life in us, transforming us more into the likeness of Christ regardless of what is happening in the work or the world to which we have gained entrance. Prayer is also what will enable us to be long-suffering in this work. Long-suffering is that power which enables us to suffer on, to bear with the suffering, to assimilate it and use it without letting it irritate, exasperate or numb us. We must learn to be long-suffering with God Himself. The strain He puts on us in this work is immense. Part of that strain results from the fact that God uses the work of counseling to do the work of redemption *in us*—to help some maimed limb *in us* recover or to exercise some impaired faculty.

When we pray, we are taught

The work we do demands much time and patience. God's methods of working seem terribly slow. *Prayer is the school in which we are shaped and molded to His design.* Prayer is the way we learn to live and walk at God's pace. God is patient because He is eternal. We are impatient because we are creatures of time. He desires to make us like Himself. Think of the waiting this work requires of us. Think of the time that passes between first hearing a victim's story and the healing that eventually comes. Think of the time it takes to see bridges formed in a shattered marriage. Think of the waiting required when working with an addict. God's waiting often makes no sense to us. How can we walk with a God who waits in the midst of horrific things unless we are students in the school of prayer?

For further thought:

We often pray only our petitions for daily needs. Consider praying also to have the mind of God about the suffering we encounter.

"Prayer is God's plan to supply man's great and continuous need with God's great and continuous abundance."

Edward M. Bounds[5]

---

[5] Edward M. Bounds, *The Reality of Prayer*, excerpted, Christian Classics Ethereal Library, http://www.ccel.org/ccel/bounds/reality.txt (accessed 21 May 2014), ch. 2, "Prayer—Fills Man's Poverty with God's Riches."

Boundaries and the Cause of Christ

As counselors, we are usually very attuned to boundary and power issues (or at least we should be). We know that counseling is a professional relationship, not a personal one, and, hence, there are certain parameters that need to be honored. In addition, we know that the therapeutic relationship puts a great deal of power in the hands of the therapist and we are never to use that power to manipulate another in order to meet our own emotional or relational needs— whether it be to inflate our wallets or feed our egos or sexual appetites. We are the therapists, they are the clients...and whatever occurs within that relationship is to be for their good. Since we are Christian counselors, our caregiving must also be for the glory of God, which means it must be Christ-like. When we start "relaxing the guidelines" (as one politician

recently said), we risk becoming arrogant, dangerous, and unethical in our approach.

Mistaking good for best

One of the causes for these abuses is when Christians get
derailed by good things that become, according to devotional
author Oswald Chambers, the enemy of the best. Perhaps
some of you have read Wess Stafford's book, *Too Small to Ignore*. This powerful book passionately advocates for the "least
of these" through hearing Wess' story of abuse at the hands of
missionaries when he was in a boarding school in West Africa. That story is a grievous example of what happens when
power is in the hands of human beings who treat a good cause
(reaching those who do not know Christ) as the ruling force,
rather than love and obedience to Jesus Christ under any and
all circumstances.

The mission under whom Wess' parents served was more
devoted to a cause than it was to Jesus Christ Himself. When
we do that, we make choices for the sake of the cause or mission rather than those in keeping with the Word and character of God. For the sake of the cause of reaching the people of
Africa (an excellent goal) and allowing the cause to dominate
the decision-making process, children were sent away as their
parents fulfilled mission objectives. Then without the protection of their mothers and fathers, many of these children were
systematically abused physically, emotionally, verbally, and
sexually on a repeated basis and commanded to maintain silence regarding this horrific sin. All of these outcomes are an
affront to a holy God—evils He abhors—and are still to this
day soul-destroying for many of Wess' classmates. The idea of
"God's cause" was used as a power tool to control and domi-

nate the people of God, resulting in ongoing sin both sanctioned and covered. In an effort to reach the souls of Africans, the souls of children were overlooked and damaged beyond imagination. *Any cause that leads us to sin—to sanction or hide sin—is an ungodly force in our lives.* A good and godly cause competed with the preeminence of Jesus Christ and became toxic to the souls of leadership, missionaries, and children.

In some of the consulting I do, I see similar things in a number of counselors. Many have great compassion for those who are suffering and coming to them out of terrible histories of trauma and abuse. Compassion is good; we are called to have compassion for it is like our God. Jesus demonstrated compassion for suffering humanity again and again. We are, in fact, not following Him unless we are compassionate.

When we make compassion our god

However, compassion, if given the reins, will often lead us to ignore important boundaries and proceed in an almost messianic way in our relationships with our counselees. Their pain and our compassion become a single, but errant, compass and the result can be a therapeutic derailment. The governance of our lives is not to be compassion, *but rather the God who is compassionate.* The difference is actually profound, for the God who is always compassionate also says we are to obey those who have rule over us. We are to walk with integrity and humility, speak truth, and recognize that He, alone, is the Messiah. When only one aspect of who God is governs, rather than the whole of God Himself, we run over many of the truths of our God, like the mission that so damaged the missionary children ruled only by the "one." Ultimately, we may end up doing great damage to people and His Name. If so, we will defame Him by looking nothing like Him...and all under the banner of His great name. How that must grieve Him! We are called to a higher standard—one that models compassion, appropriate boundaries, and ethical behavior.

For further thought:

Boundary violations always begin with tiny decisions to adopt "the good" over "the best." Ask God to show you these temptations.

———————————

"Where would you be if God took away all your Christian work? Too often it is our Christian work that is worshiped and not God."

Oswald Chambers[6]

———————————

[6] Oswald Chambers, *Disciples Indeed* in *The Complete Works of Oswald Chambers* (Grand Rapids, MI: Discovery House Publishers, 2000), p. 411, "Workers for God." Used by permission; see References.

Eyes on the Master

On a Saturday morning many years ago, my husband and I took our two boys, then seven and three, out to buy a puppy for the seven-year-old's birthday. We intended to go to a breeder but impulsively pulled into a pet store on the way just to see what they had. The owner very cleverly let an eight-week-old blond Cocker Spaniel out of her cage. She followed us everywhere with her eyes riveted on ours and her tail wagging. The two little boys were hooked (so were the parents, I must confess). She came home in a box on the back seat.

From the beginning, her love and loyalty were unquestionable. We named her Taffy (for her color), and there were a few years when her blond curls and those of her young owner would run together as one when they lay side by side on the floor. Every morning she ran up the stairs followed by mommy with orange juice, and every morning two little boys started their day with a thump on the bed and wet kisses. Her love was unquenchable. Her eyes always followed us with her tail wagging behind.

We buried her fifteen years later. The seven-year-old was already in graduate school and the three-year-old was a 6' 5" freshman in college. Even up to the end, when she could no longer get up, her cloudy eyes would follow us unflinchingly. When we buried her, my eyes were full of tears, and I thought to myself, *She did her job well for she loved us well.* "Well done, good and faithful servant!" (Matt. 25:23). I realized at that moment that the tribute given to Taffy could not be surpassed, and that I longed for nothing higher than what she was accorded.

What is the thing in this life that should outweigh all else in importance? "Love the Lord your God with all your heart and with all your soul and with all your mind and with all your strength. The second is this: 'Love your neighbor as yourself'" (Mark 12:30-31). It is easy for us as counselors, given the often critical demands of the work we do, to put the second commandment ahead of the first. The needs of people press against us. Their panic is contagious. It is not hard for us to become governed by such needs, and it is a short step from there to thinking of ourselves as indispensable.

Watch out for drifting eyes

It gets hard, doesn't it, walking deliberately into the darkness of other lives? It gets on us and in us. How quickly our eyes become riveted on the task and not the Master! We think somehow that our primary task is the work we do. It is a good work. It is an important work. It is even a work that God himself has called us to do. It is, however, never to become our main work. Our first task, the one that is to govern all else, is that of maintaining a relationship with the only One who is needful (Luke 10:42). The discipline is hard. The distractions of many good things often lead us to forget the best thing.

I enjoyed shooting arrows into targets years ago. My instructor would repeatedly say to me, "Fix your eyes, Diane." Anytime my eyes drifted from their fixed point, my arrow went off course. The writer to the Hebrews instructs us in a similar fashion: "Throw off everything that hinders, and the sin which so easily entangles. And let us run with perseverance...fixing our eyes on Jesus" (Heb. 12:1-2). Don't be fooled. Encumbrances can come in pretty packages: acclaim, success, money, grateful people. They can come in compelling packages as well: panic, depression, fear, desperation. However, make no mistake, *anything* that pulls our eyes from the One who should be our fixed point will result in our going off course.

Entangling sins bump us off course as well. They nip at our heels and often lead us to be fixed on something other than our Master—our needs or a desire for relief. C.H. Spurgeon captured it well, "No ties of friendship, no chains of beauty, no flashings of talent, no shafts of ridicule must turn me from the fixed resolve to flee from sin."[7] It has been rather humbling to be taught eternal lessons by a dog. She has left me an example I will not forget. Do I begin my mornings "bounding up the stairs" to greet my Master with love and joy? Do I keep my eager eyes fixed on Him, ever desiring to please? Will I be faithful even to the end, so that though I walk through the valley of the shadow of death (Ps. 23:4), I will remain attuned

---

[7] Charles Haddon Spurgeon, *Devotional Classics of C.H. Spurgeon: Morning & Evening*, excerpted, Grace Gems, http://gracegems.org/B/ morning_and_evening07.htm (accessed 21 May 2014), July 25, morning.

to His footsteps, using my last bit of energy to lift my head to see His face?

I must confess I was often frustrated with the "puppyness" of Taffy. She was not exactly brilliant. However, she never lost sight of what really mattered. How like God to use such a creature to teach an upright, two-legged creature with a far more capable brain what the Scriptures truly mean when they say that the eyes of the servant are riveted on her Master (Ps. 123:2).

For further thought:

Re-read Hebrews 12:1-2. Pray for your eyes not to drift from the author and perfecter of your faith.

"The love of God the motive principle, the ruling passion—the glory of God the undivided object and aim—the will no opposing or antagonist bias."

John MacDuff[8]

---

[8] John Ross MacDuff, *The Faithful Promiser* (New York: Thomas N. Stanford, 1857), p. 65.

Brief Meditation 1

"The soul is so constituted that it craves fulfillment from
things outside itself and will embrace earthly joys for satisfaction when it cannot reach spiritual ones. The believer is
in spiritual danger if he allows himself to go for any length
of time without tasting the love of Christ and savoring the
felt comforts of a Savior's presence. When Christ ceases to
fill the heart with satisfaction, our souls will go in silent
search of other lovers."

John Flavel[9]

---

[9] John Flavel, "The Method of Grace" in *The Whole Works of John
Flavel* (London: Baynes, 1820), vol. 2, p. 438. Also
http://thegospelcoalition.org/blogs/justintaylor/2011/08/04/john-flavel-
on-the-importance-of-gospel-delight

Brief Meditation 2

"Wants are my best riches,
because I have these supplied by Christ."

Samuel Rutherford[10]

---

[10]Samuel Rutherford, *Letters of Samuel Rutherford: With a Sketch of His Life and Biographical Notices of His Correspondents* (Edinburgh: Oliphant, Anderson and Ferrier, 1891), Letter CCXXII, p. 433.

Week 2

Obedience in the Seemingly Insignificant

Have you ever been struck by how radically different things are in the kingdom of God? I fear I am often lulled into thinking that what I know and how I do things is in accord with the way of God. I am a relatively rational person with a decent amount of insight so surely what I am thinking about something is the right and godly way to think.

How grateful I am that God takes the time to disabuse me of such ridiculous ideas!

Some months ago I had to spend a lot of time doing something I did not want to do. I had agreed to the thing a long time ago and my life had changed quite radically since I made that agreement. Time is a very precious commodity to me. The cost of giving that amount of time in the way called for was very sacrificial. The arena was small and hidden. The time required was way out of proportion to the importance of the thing. I was frustrated, resistant, annoyed, and condescending.

I asked God to release me. He surely knew how little time I had and would want me to use it for "important" things. Surely such a "little," inconvenient, insignificant, poor use of time was not in accord with His wisdom! God did not release me and so I went and did the thing, thinking maybe it would turn out differently than I thought. It did not. It was little and hidden and wiped out my day. I went out of sheer obedience to God, knowing that since He had not released me that I must go and go for Him. It was not until the drive home that the value of the day was revealed.

The value of the day turned out not to be in its effects on others but rather in its effect on me. God sent me to use my time in a seemingly insignificant way because of what He wanted to teach me, not what He wanted me to teach others.

He took me to James 2:1, 9: "Do not hold your faith in our glorious Lord Jesus Christ with an attitude of personal favoritism.... [I]f you show partiality you are committing sin" (NASB). I had failed to measure with God's measure. According to Him, the little and insignificant was as important as the big and "significant." The issue was not magnitude, but obedience. How often we measure by size, numbers, time, influence, and money. God's measuring stick does not have those markers on it. Our Lord Jesus Christ is "measured" an adequate Savior, though He became poor, little, despised, and among the rejected. Why? Because He was obedient to the will of the Father. I am not to show favoritism to those things which I deem significant, big, worthy or important. My favoritism is to be for obedience alone. How different from the way I usually think!

God also taught me that I am never to consider what He has done in my life and then conclude that I am superior in any way. Whether we are referring to maturity, gifts, accomplishments or anything else, I only have those things by His hand. Who He was and what He had did not result in superiority but in a likeness to us. We see such things as taking us out ahead of the pack, separating us from the rubble. In Christ, those things resulted in a turning to become like us, walk with us, and spend time with us at infinite cost.

Finally, I was reminded by God that what I did, I did for Him. What I did for the least I, in fact, did for the Most. It is a truth I teach. It was a truth I forgot. How good of God to use a circumstance to test the inclinations of my heart and hold them up against what I say I believe.

My wasted day suddenly became very precious to me. Its value had nothing to do with what I did, who was there, how much time I gave or what the results were. The value of that day was in the fact that my Father used the ordinary stuff of human life to manifest Himself to me. I, who keep trying to live in the extraordinary, find my Father showing Himself in the ordinary. He did it in creation, in a burning bush, in a tabernacle, in a Babe and in a bunch of fishermen. I see that extraordinary is never in the thing itself but rather in the presence of God in the thing. And so my ordinary, small, and hidden day became beautiful with the presence of Christ.

For further thought:

How are you being asked to become obedient in the insignificant? Look for images of Christ in these things.

"My father, do with me as thou wilt.... I am thy child, the inheritor of thy spirit.... Let me be thine in any shape the love that is my Father may please to have me."

George MacDonald[11]

---

[11] George MacDonald, *Unspoken Sermons: Series III*, excerpted, Lectionary Central, http://www.lectionarycentral.com/christmas/ GeorgeMacDonald.html (accessed 21 May 2014), "The Creation in Christ."

Vision: His or Mine?

There is a lot of discussion today about vision statements, mission statements, and the like. They seem to be the organizational buzzwords of our time. I certainly have no problem with that and believe they can be very helpful in focusing an institution and its workers.

I have, however, been struck recently by how often as Christians we seem to expect God to adapt Himself to our plans, our hopes, and our vision. We come up with an idea, a good idea, and hold it up for His blessing. We are sure to the point of impertinence sometimes that He will approve of what we want to do.

Rather than seeking Him so that He might show us what His vision is for us, for our organization and for the need in front of us, we develop one for ourselves and anticipate His nod of approval. We seem to have forgotten that God has told us, "My thoughts are not your thoughts, neither are your ways my ways.... As the heavens are higher than the earth, so are my ways higher than your ways and my thoughts than your thoughts" (Isaiah 55:8-9).

I fear we also show our arrogance in another way. We wait before God, asking for His thoughts, His vision, for the task at hand and He graciously gives it to us. We thank Him for it and then run off, sure we know exactly how to manage and carry out what He has given. His vision is done our way. We do this in organizations and institutions, in churches, and in our marriages. Do we really think we can take an idea born in the mind of God and presume we know how to carry it out? Surely He has His own thoughts and ways about the "how" of a vision He has imparted.

Submissive creatures we are not. Since our days in the Garden, we have displayed arrogance and impetuousness, often carrying out our own schemes or carrying out God's in our own ways, using His name as a stamp of approval for all we do. I have been profoundly impacted in recent days by the simple Scriptural statement found in Genesis 5:24—"Enoch walked with God" (NASB). Literally, the verse says that Enoch walked and continued to walk with God.

It occurred to me that rather than walking with God, I am often busily asking Him to walk with me. How backwards that is! God has invited me to walk with Him in His way. If I am to do so, I must go His way and walk at His pace. He determines the way in which I go, and both the speed and the process by which I get there.

I love the old hymn, Be Thou My Vision. One of the lines says, "naught be all else to me save that Thou art." All other visions are to be subservient to the vision of Christ. The vision must look like Him, the process must look like Him, and the goal must look like Him. That means that anytime my vision or my process or my goal, no matter how good, leads me to do something that is not Christ-like, it is wrong.

My musings have led me to an interesting question. I used to begin my day asking God to accompany me throughout all the things that I was facing. Of course, I do want Him to do that, and, in fact, He has promised that He will. His presence is a given, for He has said He will never leave or forsake me. I have changed the question so that I ask Him which way He is going so that I might accompany Him. The question helps to fix my eyes on Him as my Master and as the One who goes before. The question also reminds me that it is the tracks of His footsteps that determine my road without any hesitation or dispute.

May our visions, our ways, and our goals be His so that He might be glorified in all things.

For further thought:

Pray, "Lord, what are you doing in my world? Enable me to follow Your lead."

"My thoughts are not your thoughts."

Isaiah 55:8

Entering In

Our Lord frequently taught by means of parables when He was here in the flesh. Those who had ears to hear understood what He was teaching. I believe He still teaches us through parables. Our own lives, the lives of those around us and many things in the natural world bring His thoughts and His heart to us if only we have ears to hear. Sadly, we are often so busy and frantic living out our lives in this world, that like Jesus' contemporaries, we fail to really hear His voice as He walks with us and uses the stuff of our day-to-day lives to reveal Himself to us.

A glorious family vacation in Spain was full of His voice for me. Our son had spent a semester studying at the University of Barcelona and we joined him there for ten wonderful days. Spain is a beautiful country and its citizens were classy and very warm. The trip was full of memorable people and places—the Gothic quarter of Barcelona, the Benedictine monastery so high up you sometimes walked through the clouds, the medieval walled city of Gerona and Christmas Eve—all left indelible impressions.

Then there was our son's host family. They were also classy, warm, and generous. We were welcomed into their home in the Gothic quarter for a typical, multi-course Sunday dinner with extended family (including a 92-year-old grandmother). They spoke no English and, apart from our son, we spoke no Spanish. Their culture, their thinking, their manners, their language, their home, and their faith were all different from ours. And therein lay the parable.

The voice of my Master spoke through that afternoon to me. "See and experience the difference. Let yourself down into them. Do not just watch them. Try them on; enter into them." And I did. I entered into most of them freely, even eagerly (though I must admit, the prawn's eyeballs gave me a moment's pause). The differences interested me, challenged and stretched me, and changed me.

It is good to be challenged, for I find human beings (myself included) to be relentlessly egocentric. Our typical response to difference, whether it be in a spouse or another culture, is to back up and/or judge it as inferior. We are uncomfortable, even fearful, about entering in. Experiencing difference changes our lenses, humbles us, and increases not only our understanding, but also our capacity to love. Sitting in the therapist's chair for 40 years with many people who were very different from me has had a similar impact. That is a good thing.

Parables seem to have two parts to them. Often the first is about me—something I need to see, repent of, and change.

The second part is always about Him. My Master speaks again—"Do you see Me in the situation, the experience? Use it to know Me more clearly."

Ah, yes, of course, I see You. You are the One who entered into the greatest experience of difference ever. Good came down into evil. Infinite became finite; powerful became powerless. Life became death. It changed You too. You are forever nail-scarred.

Gratitude rises up. Thankfulness beyond words. Teach me to be like You, the One who enters in.

For further thought:

Where has God given you a challenge to enter in? Pray for the Spirit to enable you to enter into that place with the love and compassion of your Savior.

"Venture through the thick of all things after Christ, and lose not your Master, Christ, in the throng of this great market."

Samuel Rutherford[12]

---

[12] Samuel Rutherford, *Letters of Samuel Rutherford: With a Sketch of His Life and Biographical Notices of His Correspondents* (Edinburgh: Oliphant, Anderson and Ferrier, 1891), Letter CCLI, p. 496.

Are You Listening?

She survived the tragedy of September 11th. It was quite a story and she told it well. She talked about running down halls and sidewalks, watching people trampled. She remembered the young and wealthy dropping their expensive briefcases and computers as they fled. What was gain they counted loss.

She said that while she was fleeing for her life she felt afraid and anxious (of course). She tried very hard to remember some Bible verses. She wanted to comfort and reassure herself with them. Nothing came to mind, for her brain was not working as well as it usually did. She said this: "I could only remember His name, but it was enough."

I do not think I will ever forget that. Briefcases and computers, the stuff of busy lives, dropped and forgotten. Only He remained. And He was enough. How easy it is to lose that lesson in the midst of our busy lives. Money, work, schedules, deadlines, reputations, such things seem so crucial. But when life is threatened, they cannot save. Nor can they comfort. I pray the lesson will be burned in my soul so that I will live out of a heart that knows He is enough.

It seemed like a lot to learn from one woman's story. She, however, had not finished teaching. Have you ever noticed that the important lessons are often taught by those who have no knowledge that they are teaching? Our clients, for example. I went up to her after she finished her story to thank her for taking the time to tell it to us. She seemed surprised that I would thank her. She made a startling statement: "I am so grateful you came. I could not believe that you wanted to come just to listen. So many counselors only want to talk. They don't want to listen because they don't want the truth to get in the way of their counseling."

Words are the stuff of the trade. Words are how we do therapy. We need to know how to use them well. Words need to be under our command. It is easy, however, for those things we set out to master, to master us.

Money is like that. We set out to earn money, to own lots of it. What happens? Often those who "own" the most money are owned by that money, aren't they? Do you suppose words can do the same thing? I am afraid so. We teach and cease to be students. We listen and learn about various disorders and having mastered the information we then cease to listen to our clients and simply wax eloquent about what we have learned. When that happens, we have become those who "do not want the truth to get in the way of our counseling." We cease to enter each new life with the humility that says, "I do not know you." Teach me what it is like to be you. I want the truth of your particular life to impact me and shape the way I respond to you. When we no longer do these things, we cease to be like Christ.

God in Christ did let the truth of our world and our lives get in the way of His response to us. The truth of our world shaped His response to us. He entered into our experience with humility. He became flesh and learned what it is like to be us. He listened by becoming like us. He allowed who we are to impact Him and shape His response to us to the point of death. The truth determined His response. May we as counselors learn to listen to others as our God has listened to us, with humbly entering into and being impacted by the truth of our lives. It cost Him. It will cost us as well.

For further thought:

Ask the Lord to show you where you are prone to stop listening and learning.

"The Sovereign LORD has given me a well-instructed tongue, to know the word that sustains the weary. He wakens me morning by morning, wakens my ear to listen like one being instructed."

Isaiah 50:4

In Our Lives First

In the course of my work, I have often been brought into situations where pastors or counselors have misused the privileges and responsibilities of the positions they hold and abused or wounded one of the sheep they were tending. It never ceases to grieve me, for the damage is always greater than the deeds done. Through the years, I have noticed such cases always involve lives that are split into public and private, known and hidden.

It is an odd thing when you think about the nature of the work we do. We are always digging, exposing, calling to truth, and bringing things to the light. Yet, at the same time we are bringing light to bear on another's life, how easy it is to keep aspects of our own away from that same light. The healers are indeed in need of the same work as the wounded!

Do we really think we can bring light and life to those we counsel, teach and lead, when that light and life are relegated to public appearances in our own lives rather than impregnating the very substance of who we are? The treasure we hold is certainly contained in earthen vessels, but the outworking of that treasure in our lives is to be such that the vessel is transformed from the inside out. I fear sometimes the treasure is diluted and discolored by the taste of the vessel!

It is a rule of life that the inward affects the outward. We see this in the physical realm. You may have a disease eating away at you and not know it for some time. Eventually, however, the inward will affect the outward and the ravages of that disease will be apparent. The disease of hidden sin is no different. A person's inward nature, no matter how well hidden, tinges every word and deed that proceeds forth. Over time we can judge the secrets of the soul by their manifestations in the life.

Do we really believe we can lead another to freedom from bondage when we are enslaved to something ourselves? Do we really think we can teach another to love when we are filled with bitterness and rage toward those we have been called to love? How can we cultivate purity, holiness, patience, endurance, and self-control in the lives of those God brings to us when such things are not truly present in the recesses of our lives?

Jesus presents an astounding model for leadership. He says this: "For them I sanctify myself, that they too may be truly sanctified" (John 17:19). We must be what we would have those who follow us become. If that was true for our Lord and Master how much more so for us! The idea is not that we push and pull on others to get them to change in some aspect of their lives, but rather that we do the hard work of change as we submit to the work of the Spirit in our lives first. That means if I am to help you learn to deal with an addiction, I must ask the Spirit to work with me regarding those things in my life that own me. It means that wherever you need to go, I must be willing to go first in my own life. If I do not, though I may bring skills and techniques that may be helpful, I will not bring them infused with the life of God.

The Song of Songs speaks to these matters in the following statement: "My mother's sons were angry with me and made me take care of the vineyards; my own vineyard I have neglected" (1:6, NIV 1984). Is not counseling akin to being a caretaker in the vineyards of our God? We are called and gifted by Him to work in His place, among His people and for His glory. We have not heard Him clearly if we fail to understand that one of the requirements for that work is that it must go on continually in us as well. If it does not, while we may appear for a time to be doing His work, eventually what is true will be made manifest—that we have not, for the sake of others, bent to the sanctification process ourselves. We will damage His world, His people, and His Name. May it never be so.

For further thought:

Pray, "Lord, let no public/private split happen in me. Shine Your light in my soul to show me what is not of You. By Your grace, transform me into Your likeness."

"How can you say to your brother, 'Let me take the speck out of your eye,' when all the time there is a plank in your own eye?"

Matthew 7:4

Brief Meditation 3

"In proportion as he is precious to us, will be our aversion to sin and all unholiness.... From sincere love to Jesus Christ, will arise hatred of those things which are contrary to his will, and which oppose and hinder us in our endeavors after conformity to him."

John Fawcett[13]

---

[13] John Fawcett, *Christ Precious to Those Who Believe*, excerpted, Grace Gems, http://gracegems.org/28/fawcett_christ_precious3.htm (accessed 21 May 2014), Part 2, ch. 3, section 9, para. 1 and 4.

Brief Meditation 4

"The reason our affections are so chilled and cold in religion—is that we do not warm them with thoughts of God. Hold a magnifying glass to the sun, and the glass burns that which is near to it. So when our thoughts are lifted up to Christ, the Sun of righteousness, our affections are set on fire... O saints, do but let your thoughts dwell upon the love of Christ, who passed by angels and thought of you; who was wounded that, out of his wounds, the balm of Gilead might come to heal you; who leaped into the sea of his Father's wrath, to save you from drowning in the lake of fire!"

Thomas Watson[14]

---

[14] Thomas Watson, *The Great Gain of Godliness,* 1681, Part 2.

Week 3

The Beginning of Deception

Have you ever thought about how much of the work of counseling has to do with deception—often many layers of it?

Think about all the lies we fight against in the lives of those who come to see us: the lies others have told them, the lies they tell themselves, the lies from the surrounding culture, the lies they have somehow wrapped up in Scripture. Given that the Word of God tells us that our enemy is the father of lies, it would seem that a great deal of counseling is about struggling with the litter of the enemy of our souls in those who come to see us. Of course, part of the problem is that he has littered in our lives as well, which means we are vulnerable to being deceived and then misleading those who look to us for wisdom.

Splitting: The Root of Deception

There are many mechanisms for deception in a human heart. I have spent a lot of time recently thinking about one in particular. That is how we split off a very, very small part of ourselves from the truth or the light and let it continue untouched, thinking it is hurting no one (obviously a major deception!). It can start in a seemingly innocuous way and, if left unexposed to the light and transformed, can eventually end up in an out-of-control sexual addiction, a broken home or even genocide.

This fallen, unjust, and hurtful world brings us "invitations" to split on a daily basis. We can so easily tuck away a little resentment, bitterness, grudge, bit of envy or greed or lust. We feel justified in feeling it and justified in folding it up in a little corner so we can take it out and look at it every once in a while. This tucking away is the genesis of the split.

It is ever so small, but it is radioactive, and ever so lethal. You see, once you have opened and maintained a file for something, it is so easy to just tuck "one more thing" into it— she hurt me again, how can they keep doing that, I want that, or just one more look.

According to Webster (one of my favorite resources), the word "split" means to divide or separate from end to end or into layers. When the previously mentioned "things" are split off, they are hidden from public view and are left unchallenged—not just by others or by new data, but also by the Word of God and the Spirit of God. That Word and that Spirit have a great deal to say about things like resentment, bitterness, envy or lust.

Certainly that is, in part, because they have no basis in the character of God. I am sure it is also because God knows how quickly the little file becomes big and finally becomes that which governs us. Little resentments collected over time lead us to conclude that our self-justification is indeed just, and the other is not only bad, but also hopeless and someone we are right to get rid of. The little cracks become layers and, as time goes on, we split end to end.

Think about some of the marriages that we were sure were solid and godly, but one day just blew up. Think about some of the Christian leaders that we were certain were godly and then they split end to end. Think about a country like Rwanda where people named the name of Christ, attended church and school together, and then there was genocide.

We tend to be shocked at the end-to-end split. We think it makes no sense. It seems to come out of nowhere. It did not; it came from a little-by-little tucking away, hidden-from-the-light process of deception. It came from accepting as true that which was false—my resentment, my lust, or my envy is just, and I am right to hold on to it.

In Psalm 4:2 God says, "How long will my honor become a reproach [or be insulted]? How long will you love what is worthless and aim at deception?" (NASB). We certainly insult the honor of God when we think we can tuck things that are an affront to Him and His loving heart away from His sight. We are blatantly disagreeing with Him and His Word. We are dishonoring His character. We are playing the fool to think we can deceive Him as we deceive others.

If we nurture our own little splits and justify those things that are unlike Him that lie deep within our hearts, we will not work wisely or safely with others. We must remain whole—or beg God to make us whole again. I pray we as counselors will be those who honor God in the secret places, whose hidden "files" are full of His thoughts and, therefore, can lead others into a whole life, full of light from end to end.

For further thought:

We nurture splits when we accept as true what is false, when we justify or minimize sinful thoughts and feelings. Write down your temptations to split or hide parts of yourself.

"What the Christian man really is in the home circle, in the street and market, in society, in public, depends, in the order of grace, with an intense sequence and connection, upon what he is, upon what the Lord is to him, when he is quite alone."

H. C. G. Moule[15]

[15] H. C. G. Moule, *Life in Christ and for Christ* (New York: A. C. Armstrong and Son, 1890), pp. 31-32.

Some Thoughts on Repentance

Forgiveness is a popular topic today. Who would have believed that we would be reading about forgiveness in the professional literature? The world has decided that something God calls us to is good!

There is something else God calls us to that we do not hear much about, certainly not in the professional literature, but sadly, not even that much in the church. We do not hear much about repentance, do we? In consulting with a church about some difficult matters, I was asked to set forth for them what repentance actually looks like in a life. It was a profound exercise. I found it both sobering and convicting. I also realized how central it is to the work we do as counselors.

Think how healing true repentance would be for victims of sexual abuse, for those whose spouses have had affairs, for relationships ravaged by addictions. And think how damaging and confusing it is when someone who has been wounded and sinned against receives a verbal "I'm sorry" that is nothing more than words without substance.

I would like to give you, in this meditation and the next, what I have learned about repentance. God knows we need to understand it for our own lives. I learned long ago that you cannot teach another what you do not truly know yourself. You cannot lead others where you will not go. We do a disservice, or worse, further damage, if we work with those who have sinned or been sinned against without a true understanding of what repentance looks like.

Let us consider what repentance might look like for someone in leadership who carried on a sexual relationship with someone under his or her care. The first question is an important one. Of what does the person need to repent? We tend, I think, to answer the question on a superficial or merely behavioral level. We do a great disservice to the person we are working with and demonstrate a naiveté about sin when this is so. In our example, we are faced with at least the following: adultery, deceit and lies, rebellion, hypocrisy, presumption, stealing, lust, and unfaithfulness to God, spouse, and the body of Christ.

What does repentance look like?

What is the nature of repentance? The word means "to have another mind" about something. It really means to have the mind of Christ about the sin(s) we have committed. I formerly had my own thoughts about the sin, but having repented, I now have another mind, i.e., the mind of Christ. At the very least, repentance will include the following:

- truth about the sin, the events surrounding it, my-self, and its impact on others;
- humility, a submissive spirit. I will recognize that I have demonstrated a lack of wisdom and discern-ment. Having demonstrated the "wrong mind," I will be humble enough to submit myself to those who give evidence of the mind of Christ;
- empathy for those who have been wronged and damaged by my sin;
- an awareness that the sin is against the goodness and holiness of God, not merely a behavioral aber-ration that got me in trouble;
- a desire to make restitution.

Paul says, "Godly sorrow brings repentance that leads to salvation...See what this godly sorrow has produced in you: what earnestness, what eagerness to clear yourselves, what indignation, what alarm, what longing, what concern, what readiness to see justice done" (2 Cor. 7:10-11a).

Is the person diligent to deal with his or her sin? Is the per-son eager to be rid of all complicity with sin in his or her life? Is the person greatly afflicted with the offender, i.e., him- or herself? Is the person alarmed by his or her susceptibility to the sin? Does he or she long for restoration? Does he or she demonstrate zeal for God's honor? Does he or she strenuously work for a clearing of the sin and its consequences?

It is easy to see why I was both sobered and convicted by my study. Such fruit in a life is not born of counseling tech-niques, though God may use them. The fruit of repentance is the work of the Spirit of God in a life. May those of us who counsel others seek its cleansing work where necessary. We who have seen how sin ravages lives should be the first on our knees.

For further thought:

We silence the Spirit when we make excuses for affections that exist in us that do not come from God. Pray for God to reveal those places and to leave no false thing behind.

———————————————

"Create in me a pure heart, O God, and renew a steadfast spirit within me."

Psalm 51:10

Evidences of True and False Repentance

epentance is defined by Paul as an intensely godward sorrow that fashions transformation (2 Cor. 7:10). How easily we slide into seeing it, not as godward but as "humanward." And how readily we reduce it to words and tears rather than transformation.

One of the Puritans, Obadiah Sedgwick (who else would have such a name!), wrote an excellent book, *The Anatomy of Secret Sins*. He gives us four things that give evidence of a superficial repentance, which is, of course, no repentance at all.

The first is that the principal restraint is only for those things that fall under the eyes of others. This results in restraining sin *so it is not visible.*

Second, that which grieves the person reveals that which owns the heart. Those who grieve loss of position or reputation love their work more than their God.

Third, when the sin in the heart is not the real burden—
but rather the specific consequences are seen as the greater
burden, e.g., loss of job, reactions of others—then repentance
is not deep.

And finally, when we care more about being spared than
about being truly searched by the Word of God and the Spirit
of God, we are not truly desirous of being cleansed from sin.
When the Holy Spirit convicts of sin (as opposed to our simply getting caught), it is not our relationships with others that
trouble us primarily (though trouble us they should), but our
relationship with God.

Think about what repentance is and what it is not in the
context of counseling a Christian leader who has fallen, a bat-
terer, or someone caught in an addiction to Internet pornography. Truly it is a difficult thing to repent. It is hard, deep
work, and we shortchange our clients when we do not understand this and fail to do everything we can to help them repent. Sedgwick says it is not "easy for a man to become an
enemy to himself, to lay down his sweet delight," his natural
bent, and to "condemn his heart and ways...forsake his own
counsels and inclinations."[16] Charles Spurgeon tells us that
true repentance is recognizable by the fact that the repentant
one dreads the sin "as the burnt child dreads fire."[17] Oswald
Chambers teaches that repentance "destroys the lust of self-
vindication" and that "wherever that lust resides, repentance is

---

[16] Obadiah Sedgwick, *Anatomy of Secret Sins, Presumptuous Sins, Sins in Do-
minion and Uprightness* (London: Printed by T.R. for A. Byfeild, 1660), p. 96.
[17] Charles Haddon Spurgeon, *Devotional Classics of C.H. Spurgeon: Morning &
Evening*, excerpted, Grace Gems, http://gracegems.org/B/morning_
and_evening10.htm (accessed 21 May 2014), October 13, morning.

not true."[18] Such teachings help us to see how rare the jewel of true repentance is.

Repentance and the work of the counselor

How do these truths relate to our counseling practices? First of all, I think it is very easy for us to get so caught up in the clinical aspects of our work that we fail to tend to matters of the heart. I believe that our clinical work is important. There is a body of knowledge we should know thoroughly and skills we should perform with excellence. To be poorly versed or sloppy in such matters is wrong and does not glorify the God we serve. However, to think our clinical knowledge is sufficient for working with the hearts and lives of human beings is foolish.

Second, we cannot foster true repentance in the lives of our clients unless it is a reality in our own. How can we expect to recognize superficial repentance or nurture true repentance if we have never bowed the knee and allowed God to do that work in our own hearts?

Paul, in Galatians 6:1, says, "If someone is caught in a sin, you who live by the Spirit should restore him gently. But watch yourself, or you also may be tempted." I take from this Scripture the following: (1) Those involved in restoration, as we certainly are, should be those who live lives of repentance, bear the fruit of the Spirit in their lives, and have the mind of Christ; (2) Restoration is to be done with humility; there is no room for harshness, superiority, or disdain; and (3) Restoration is accompanied by watchfulness. Sin is contagious. It is

---

[18] Oswald Chambers, *Conformed to His Image* in *The Complete Works of Oswald Chambers* (Grand Rapids, MI: Discovery House Publishers, 2000), p. 349. Used by permission; see References.

easy to catch the disease you are working with or react to one sin with another, e.g., pride or a critical spirit.

Repentance is a work begun and carried out by the Spirit of God. It is neither quick nor easy. It is far more than words and emotion. When it is not present in a client, our call is to intercede for that person until it is. To engage in such work is to stand on holy ground. I have never gone through this process with another where God has not used it to convict me of sin as well. His call to us as counselors is to respond to our sin in the way we would lay out for others. May we be counselors who are not merely concerned with the health of our clients but with their holiness as well.

For further thought:

Meditate on the features of superficial repentance found in one of your clients. Ask the Lord to teach you something about your own need for godly sorrow.

———

"Genuine, spiritual mourning for sin is the work of the Spirit of God. Repentance is too choice a flower to grow in nature's garden. Pearls grow naturally in oysters, but penitence never shows itself in sinners except divine grace works it in them. If thou hast one particle of real hatred for sin, God must have given it thee, for human nature's thorns never produced a single fig."

Charles Spurgeon[19]

———

[19] Charles Haddon Spurgeon, *Devotional Classics of C.H. Spurgeon: Morning & Evening*, excerpted, Grace Gems, http://gracegems.org/B/morning_and _evening10.htm (accessed 21 May 2014), October 13, morning.

Shepherding with Integrity

I have been thinking a lot about integrity lately. In part, I suppose, because I have had several messy situations cross my path that demonstrated a lack of integrity. The wife of a man whose public and private selves were the antithesis of each other said, "It hurts so much when someone's inside and outside do not match." Like me, I am sure you have worked with lives that have lacked integrity and you have seen the disastrous results. These results seem to multiply when the person has been in a leadership position. The wreckage reverberates through communities, institutions, and families.

The word integrity means "whole, upright, an unbroken state, unimpaired." To have integrity is to be the same all the way through. To have integrity means no part of me is folded up, hidden away out of sight. To have integrity means wholeness under pressure, to not split apart. That's the key, for pressure is often applied to test something, to see if it will hold up. Our lives are full of pressure. Are we constant under that pressure, or do we split something off for ourselves because, after all, "no one could be expected to remain honest, faithful, loving, or self-controlled under those circumstances"?

There is great pressure in our culture that encourages us to split. In a reference to politicians, Jay Rosen, a NYU media scholar said, "There is an important distinction between public and private character. What candidates do in private is largely irrelevant. What matters is their public conduct" (Quoted by Jeromy Iggers, Minneapolis Star Tribune, 1992). In other words, the only part of you that matters is the part that is seen in public.

There are many personal things that bring pressure on our lives. Limited time, excessive demands, work, family, suffering, and expectations all push on us in varying ways. We get weary; we need rest. There are also significant factors in the counseling office that bring pressure to bear on us. Counseling is a very intimate relationship, often charged with emotional intensity and laced with power dynamics. That is a lot of pressure on one frail human being! Add to that mix the fact that it is a financial arrangement. It does not take a counseling degree to know what money can do to people. And finally, the work of counseling, particularly with certain issues or types of clients, can be very depleting. The potential to split apart, to pretend, to deceive, can be great. How easy to slide into unethical behavior, to begin to "care" for ourselves in destructive ways. How easy it is to begin in some fashion to feed on the sheep, using them to feel better, more important, heard, powerful, and successful.

The psalmist says: "David shepherded them with integrity of heart; with skillful hands he led them" (Ps. 78:72). He guided those who were under his care for God's glory and their good, not for his own glory and good. His skill was executed wisely, not only in word but also in deed. But wait! Isn't this the man who once took the poor man's lamb? (2 Sam. 12:4). Yes, it is. It is the king who fed on his sheep rather than protected them. It is the shepherd who split apart and acted without integrity. But when David's lack of integrity was uncovered, he did not point to circumstances for an explanation. He did not blame the pressures of his life. He simply said, "I have sinned against the Lord." And then later he cried to God, "Create in a me a pure heart [unimpaired, unbroken], O God, and renew a steadfast spirit [faithfulness, integrity] within me" (Ps. 51:10).

May we be like David, shepherding with integrity the people who come to us. May we not be moved by the pressures of life to split apart. And may we remember that the source of integrity is not discipline, effort, or determination, though these will be involved in its exercise. The source of integrity is the only one who can create pure hearts out of faithless ones, the great I AM. He who is unchanging, who is faithful and true, calls us to walk before Him, daily seeking His face, so as to be transformed into His image, that of a shepherd who tends His flock, gathers His lambs, carries them close to His heart and gently leads (Isa. 40:11). That shepherd carried His lambs all the way to Calvary and did not split apart. May we follow Him even there.

For further thought:

Take a moment to name some of the pressures in your life this week. Ask God to reveal His power and mind about these pressures and thank Him for His steadfast care.

"Teach me your way, LORD, that I may rely on your faithfulness; give me an undivided heart, that I may fear your name."

Psalm 86:11

DAY 19

Lured from Within

People come to us to deal with all kinds of external situations and difficult people in their lives. We help them face abuse, loss, sickness, injustice, and relational struggles. Life on this planet can be hard and dark.

You and I are called upon to minister to those who are suffering, and walk with them as they wrestle. People also come to us, sometimes unknowingly, to deal with themselves. Sin and self-deception are as integral a part of the work of people-helping as is suffering. I fear we often fail to see the whole picture and fall out into one of two camps.

Some of us major on external suffering and its impact on the lives of those we see and we fail to consider what is happening in the sinful heart before us. Others go on a sin-hunt, assuming there is always an internal cause for the suffering and if we can just figure it out, then we can get rid of the suffering. Wisdom dictates that we must consider both and that the intertwining of the two can lead to a mind-boggling complexity in a human life.

I have been thinking recently about sin and how it destroys lives. It is often called by a different name than what it actually is. It is also frequently blamed on external circumstances. We think that the suffering, the sin of another, the pain, or the allurement of an external object are really the causes of our sin.

We rarely look to ourselves for the cause, to our own sin as the root of our trouble. I encountered such thinking in someone recently, and in my struggle to help them see some truth about themselves, I spent time studying James 1:14-16. It was both fascinating and convicting.

James teaches that temptation is a way of being tested in order to validate what we really think or feel. It is, in essence, an exposure technique. I can say I am not tempted to anger, but such a claim is validated only when someone crosses my boundaries, offends me or treats me unjustly. Whether or not I am angry will be exposed in the process. He goes on to say that we are baited, lured, deceived or dragged away by our own inner cravings or coveting impulses.

In other words, we build and bait our own traps! How contrary that is to our thinking. We see ourselves as being lured or dragged away by the person or situation external to us. The Scriptures, however, actually say the thing that lures us is within. It is an impulse or craving that resides inside us. Lust for something is both the source and the agent. It lures and it carries.

So often we think of lust as simply a sexual thing. Oswald Chambers defines it as, "I must have it at once." It can be importance, approval, fame, love, money, order, reputation, attention, or any number of things. We are in bondage to the thing we must have. It is that internal thing that makes something external attractive or necessary.

Clearly, the old thinking that a rape occurred because of a short skirt is fallacious. The short skirt tells us something about the woman. The rape does not tell us about the woman, but about the rapist. Jesus teaches us the same principle when He says, "The things that proceed out of the mouth come from the heart, and those defile the man" (Matt. 15:18, NASB). The source of the defilement is internal, not external.

James goes on to say that when our own lust has delivered us as a prisoner, it produces, or gives birth to, sin. Sin is a missing of the mark, a failure to be Christ-like, and it is pregnant with death. Death is a place of darkness, silence, and captivity. Such words give one pause.

The source of the defilement is within, not without. I am lured by, and carried away by, things which reside in me. Those things lead to a failure to be like Jesus in this world in some way, and the result is death. This is about things we gravely minimize—harsh words when people push on us, manipulative words to get approval or attention, "small" deceptions to cover our tracks, or the blaming of another for our sin.

Such things expose something about who we are. Such things lead to death, darkness, and captivity. No wonder James implores us, "Do not be deceived [or seduced away from the truth], my beloved" (James 1:16, NASB). Such deception leads to destruction.

We do our clients a terrible disservice if we do not consider these things. Certainly, sin-hunts and verses used like projectiles are terrible misuses of the Word of God. However, to fail to explore and gently expose sin is to leave prisoners in bondage. That would be quite unlike our Savior who came to set the captives free!

For further thought:

In what areas in your life do you feel the pull of lust? What thing do you feel you "must have at once"? What situations and temptations reveal this internal pull?

"Temptation and occasions put nothing into a man, but only draw out what was in him before."

John Owen[20]

----

[20] John Owen, *The Golden Book of John Owen*, "Of Temptation" (London: Hodder and Stoughton, 1904), p. 156.

Brief Meditation 5

"Jesus prescribes no form of prayer... [T]he same form of prayer or fast or almsgiving might come either from love or selfishness. The same spiritual house may be built either on the rock or on the sand. To Him the foundation is everything, the superstructure quite subordinate.... He fears nothing so much as 'false prophets'—outward virtues springing from selfish motives. He fears such virtues not only because they deceive the world but because they deceive their possessor."

George Matheson[21]

---

[21] George Matheson, *Studies of the Portrait of Christ* (New York: A. C. Matheson, 1903), vol. 1, pp. 206-207.

Brief Meditation 6

"May I make it my grand ambition to be marking, day by day...my growing conformity to the holy character of a holy God. For this end, overrule all the dispensations of Thy providence. May I hear a voice in each of them proclaiming, "Be holy." May I be led to bear them all, and to rejoice in them all, if they thus be the means of bringing me nearer Thyself."

John Ross MacDuff[22]

---

[22] John Ross MacDuff, *The Morning Watches and Night Watches* (New York: Robert Carter and Brothers, 1855), pp. 19-20.

Week 4

The Crucible of Therapy

Parenting contained some epiphanies for me. One of those occurred many years ago when our sons were very small. The three-year-old chose one evening to be relentlessly disobedient about something—I no longer remember what. The youngest was still nursing, and I was a very tired young mother. I kept dragging myself upstairs with my firstborn, determined to be as relentless in training as he was in disobedience. After several trips I sat wearily on the steps and thought, "So, who is getting discipline here anyway?" I realized, of course, that the answer was both of us. Certainly I was parenting the child. However, there was another parent training another child simultaneously—my heavenly Father was training me.

I have found the process of therapy to be quite similar. In fact, both parenting and therapy have served as crucibles in my life. The word "crucible" has two meanings. First, it is a metal container used to heat substances to high temperatures. Second, it is a severe test causing lasting change. Applied personally, I am hard to manage, stubbornly disobedient at times, and I often struggle to retain my sinful shape even when heated to high temperatures. Many times high temperatures are what have revealed my shape.

The ambiguous and repetitious nature of therapy has often revealed arrogance, impatience, and judgment in me. Among my clients, demandingness, self-absorption, and resistance to treatment often make me want to quit. Blindness, self-deception, and a preference for darkness weary me. Such things serve as a crucible, heating me to high temperatures, and revealing my heart, a most uncomfortable process.

Think about it for a moment. We enter counseling with stated motives of caring for others and assisting change. Our training and ethics shape us to serve the clients' goals and not our own. The focus is on what the client needs to grow, and the process is considered successful when that growth occurs.

Until recent years, the person of the therapist was not even part of the discussion. I heard little to nothing about the nurture and care for the therapist during my graduate school days. Don't get me wrong; the care of the client is foremost. The counseling relationship does not exist to serve the needs of the therapist. When it is used in such a fashion abuse occurs. The needs and concerns of the therapist need to be met outside of counseling. We need to feed, yes, but we are not to feed off the sheep.

However, God does not confine Himself to human categories and weaknesses. He does graciously use our efforts and our interventions redemptively in the lives of our clients. Yet I have come to see that He is just as busy using the process of "helping others" to work on me. Doing therapy for 40 years has been a severe test that has produced lasting change in my life.

Many clients have asked me to enter worlds I do not desire to inhabit or even visit. They take me into worlds of abuse, violence, death, and darkness. They have often been deeply scarred by such things and bring those influences into a relationship with me. From this crucible I have seen glimpses of the humility of our God, who entered our world through the womb of a peasant girl and graced many small things with the beauty of His presence.

I have tasted His infinite patience as He has taught me how to be like Him to those who need to rework ground again and again before they taste freedom. He has taught me about His pursuit of those in darkness. I would rather sit in the light and invite them in, not go into the darkness to bring them light.

In essence, God has used the crucible of therapy to make me more like Jesus Christ. There is no doubt that high temperatures still await me for I have a great deal more to learn. I am, however, grateful for the fact that God is not boxed in by my categories. He is constantly and graciously using my time with those He has called me to serve as a crucible in my life.

It has not escaped my notice that the word "crucible" comes from the same root in Latin for the word "cross." Certainly the cross qualifies as high temperatures or a severe test that brought about lasting change. Once again, He calls us to follow Him, for He never asks us to go where He has not preceded us.

For further thought:

Pray that you will not simply view the work you do according to human categories. So much awaits us if we will allow the Refiner to do His work. Ask Him to give you eyes to see it.

"No discipline seems pleasant at the time, but painful. Later on, however, it produces a harvest of righteousness and peace for those who have been trained by it."

Hebrews 12:11

Protecting Souls with Therapeutic Confrontation

I have spent my career studying, listening to, and working with the issues that surround trauma and abuse. It began with first understanding the impact these events have on victims and then moved to considering their impact on therapists (for obvious reasons!). Later on, I began thinking through the actual world of the perpetrator, for one cannot engage in evil without increasing one's blindness and deadness. Recently, due to several situations, I have been looking more deeply at what is required by God in the character of the person who is willing to confront such evil. It is not a new topic for me, but one that has many layers and one I desire to plumb more deeply.

Galatians 6:1 says this:

"Brethren, even if anyone is caught in any trespass, you who are spiritual, restore such a one in a spirit of gentleness;

each one looking to yourself, so that you too will not be tempted" (NASB).

There are two things that often happen to us when we are dealing with another's sins. First, we know sin is a contaminant; a toxin; a cancer. We also know it can be contagious. Any time we are working with it, especially up close, we are at great risk of catching some of the "disease." Certainly we can do that by catching the same form that sits in front of us. It is, however, usually more subtle than that. Paul is essentially saying; do not come to this interaction already contaminated. The phrase "you who are spiritual" means that those who are working with the fallen one are to be, in the flesh, what he described in chapter 5:22-23. In other words, come to the sick room full of health. Come to this task with the character of one who looks like Jesus Christ. That means those who function as "restorers" must be mature believers with an evident history of walking closely to Christ.

Confront to restore?

I fear that more often than not, we tend to confront rather than restore because we are in a particular position in the Church. Paul does not mention position, and being in church leadership sadly does not insure Christ-likeness. Or sometimes we approach these issues propelled by our feelings of indignation, outrage, hurt or grief. These feelings may be appropriate in certain situations, but they are not qualifiers. The only qualifier is our character, because Paul knows we will do damage to others and/or ourselves if we have not learned that love and obedience to Jesus Christ must govern all else in every situation.

Truth and love?

Second, Paul not only wants us to enter into this role as healthy caregivers, he also wants us to remain healthy. Sometimes, we are at risk for handling another's sin at both ends of the spectrum—either with arrogance and self-righteousness or with tolerance and compromise. We might go even further and deceive ourselves by defining the first response as speaking the language of truth and the second the language of love—elements that should, in their right form, adorn any confrontation. Paul says to enter into this process by first observing yourself. Come healthy; proceed meekly. He wants us to proceed but not in anger or excessive passion. He does not want us to withdraw ourselves from the burdens which the sins committed by others might impose upon us. He wants us to sit through the process without impatience or resentment. And we are to do all of this watching ourselves carefully lest we get derailed—by anger, discouragement, bitterness, injury, or weariness—thereby losing our health by catching the disease of sin in our efforts to restore another diseased soul.

If we come in this way, protected and governed by the Spirit of God, we will be in a better position to neither ignore the sin nor do damage to the sinner or ourselves. We will enter with gentleness to repair any wounds and mend that which is broken or out of joint. By the grace and power of God, we will pass on to the fallen brother the health of the life of Christ rather than contaminating ourselves with the disease of sin. So, counselors, as you work with those who have been caught by sin, you who qualify as full of likeness to Christ, work to mend the brokenness of your dislocated counselees, carefully watching yourself so that you, too, will not be contaminated by sin.

So as we once again consider this work that we are privileged to do, we find that while we thought its main purpose was the care of others, our God is always first pursuing and working with us who are His instruments. He knows the substance with which we work. He knows well that the substance lies in us and not just our clients. He calls us yet again to Himself—the only One who lived in this sin-stricken world uncontaminated—until He took upon Himself the awful cancer and it eroded His life to death. He has instructed us in this work because He knows how this toxin can kill the soul. May we heed His Word and observe ourselves as we work.

For further thought:

With whom are you prone to truth without love; love without truth? Do not hold onto any anger, bitterness, or weariness that puts you at risk for injury.

"Sin entertained, trifled with, even treated with indifference, soon draws a dense veil between us and His presence. And conversely, His holy presence, entertained, welcomed, sought, remembered, worshiped will be the effectual anesthetic to temptation."

H. C. G. Moule[23]

---

[23] H. C. G. Moule, *High Priestly Prayer: A Devotional Commentary on the Seventeenth Chapter of St. John* (London: The Religious Tract Society, 1908), p. 102-103.

Resistance and Responsiveness

We have been discussing resistance a lot around the office lately. It has been considered in a staff meeting, in many case consultations, and even in the kitchen.

As you know from your own experience, it is a frequent occurrence in the counseling office and often a difficult thing with which to deal. It shows up in a variety of forms. Resistance can be passive, aggressive, verbal, behavioral, emotional or financial. It can be a projection into the therapeutic relationship of the patient's internal world in the form of chaos, silence or overwhelming emotion. It can be an expression of the client's relational experience with others such as ridicule, criticism or anger. The recipient of all this resistance is, of course, the therapist.

Resistance is an expression to the therapist of the client's major defense mechanism. It is something that infects all of his relationships and functions destructively in his life. Whatever he is doing "out there" relationally, he will eventually do in the counseling relationship.

It goes something like this: the client comes for counseling and you assess the situation and think you understand the issues. You see ways you might be helpful and proceed to establish an alliance and begin to help. Somewhere along the way you slam into a wall. You have met resistance in some form. Your response, then, is to try to remove the obstacle so the issues can be dealt with and change can occur.

Your client agrees with your assessment. And although he wants your help, he also wants to leave the obstacle intact. For example, you and the client agree that he has difficulty with communication and intimacy in relationships. He wants you to help him grow and change so that relationships are satisfying and healthy. As you work with him, you keep encountering silence and withdrawal. You want him to learn not to retreat into silence. He wants satisfying relationships and intimacy, but also wants to hold on to the protection afforded him by silence and withdrawal in case he needs it.

It is at this point that therapists can get frustrated, befuddled, and irritated and struggle with thoughts of inadequacy. Resistance assails the therapist's ego and produces anxiety. It derails our messianic notions and dreams of being the hero. Young therapists think it means they picked the wrong field and are not fit for the profession. Older, or sometimes weary, therapists can withdraw emotionally or react with anger or frustration. It is easy to act as if somehow the resistance is an attack against us. We misunderstand resistance.

Resistance, first and foremost, is not about the therapist. It is not a commentary or judgment of your therapeutic skill or acumen. We forget that therapy is in many ways about exposure. Thinking we have a good treatment plan, we proceed, but sometimes the resistance we encounter is surprising.

Resistance, second of all, is always there. If it is not there yet, it is coming; it will show up. It is, in fact, where the real work of therapy will happen. How is that? Because the resistance exposes the heart of the matter if you expect it, learn to sit with it, and embrace it. The wise therapist always expects it, learns to "read" it, and reflects on it.

By doing this, you will find that the resistance will teach you a great deal about your client. It will teach you something about what they want more than the overt solution or help they came to find. We resist because we fear something more than we want something new. We resist because we hold tightly to something that feels safe and protective, while all the time it is destroying or blocking that for which we long.

We really *do* understand resistance—will learn to read and decipher it correctly—if we will stop and think about it because the truth is this: *God encounters resistance in His relationship with us all the time.*

Resistance, ultimately, is an exposé of the heart. Jesus says to us, "Follow Me." We say to Him, let me first go try out my oxen or bury my father. At one level we do want change. Every one of us wants to be His disciple; we want to grow in His ways. But as we move toward Him and the transformation of our lives, the obstacles to that growth are revealed. The resistance on our part toward God reveals our hearts, our fears, and our true loves.

Furthermore, as with therapists, our resistance to God says nothing about Him, and everything about us. What reveals God to us is His response to our resistance. He does not respond with anger or withdrawal or force or condemnation. He waits, He invites, He has compassion. God understands and sometimes He is saddened, as with the rich young ruler who walked away. Loving patience is the hallmark of God's responsiveness.

We can learn from God how to respond to our clients. We can also learn from our clients something of what we do to the heart of our God when we resist Him. May His exposé of our hearts lead us to repentance and renewal, rather than an escalation of the resistance.

For further thought:

When you meet client resistance and are tempted by thoughts of inadequacy, remember that God is at work through defenses and is not thwarted by them.

"He pleads with us, and waits to be gracious to us. Admirable indeed is the longsuffering of the Saviour in bearing with some of us year after year, notwithstanding our provocations, rebellions, and resistance of his Holy Spirit. Wonder of wonders that we are still in the land of mercy!"

Charles Spurgeon[24]

---

[24] Charles Haddon Spurgeon, *Devotional Classics of C.H. Spurgeon: Morning & Evening*, excerpted, Grace Gems, http://gracegems.org/B/morning_and _evening12.htm (accessed 21 May 2014), December 31, morning.

Understanding the Trauma Survivor

People often comment about the resiliency of children when they are facing devastating circumstances such as divorce, death of a parent or abuse. Somehow the comment makes everyone feel better. Unfortunately, it is not true. To be resilient means that when something happens, you return back to your original emotional and cognitive shape. That would mean a child becomes who they were before the traumatic event took place. An abused child does not become as if he or she were never abused. A child who loses a parent never returns to being the child who had that parent. Children are in fact not resilient; they are malleable. To be malleable means you can be shaped; you are adaptable. A malleable object is one that can be pounded or pressed into another shape without returning to its original form.

This of course makes sense when you think about what a child really is. A child is growing, unfinished, developing, maturing and learning. Each of those words implies that the child can be shaped or is malleable. We concern ourselves with a child's education, nutrition, and habits because we know this principle. We want them to learn good study habits, eat healthy foods, get exercise, and develop good personal habits as well. Parents, knowingly or not, are constantly shaping their children. We understand malleability.

Hebrews 13:1, 3 says this: "Keep on loving each other...[R]emember those in prison as if you were their fellow prisoners [or as if you were bound with them]; and those who suffer as if you yourselves were suffering" (NIV 1984). If we are to understand the belief system of an adult survivor of sexual abuse, then we must comprehend the malleability of children and enter into the experience of their childhood suffering as if we had been abused. If we do not understand, we cannot help.

Let's say at some point in your counseling practice you are confronted by a woman in her 30s who tells you that she was sexually abused by her father for 15 of her growing up years. Her mother knew and never said a word. She has decided to come for counseling because her life is falling apart. She has never told anyone before. She is depressed, anxious, and cannot sleep. She has terrible nightmares. She can hardly function, her husband is upset, and she is finding it difficult to care for her children. What is it you need to understand about her?

The verse in Hebrews says, "Keep in mind those who are suffering as if you were suffering the identical thing." What would you be like, what would you need if you shared this woman's history? This woman's mother knew she was being abused and did nothing. What do you think that taught her? How might she be feeling having just told you her story? What do you think she thinks and feels about herself? What might she fear that you think about her now that you know?

She is depressed and sleep deprived. What happens to our minds when we do not get enough sleep? How well do you think she is processing? Think back to a time when you had to function without sleep. What do you think it might be like to get into bed at night, utterly exhausted, next to a man, and then spend the night having nightmares one after another of your father raping you? How do you suppose she might feel about sex with her husband? Do you think she might want to die, or hurt herself, or ingest any substance she can find in order to keep going or get some sleep?

What do you suppose she thinks about God? Do you think she is confident that God loves her or that He protects her or that she matters to Him? Do you think it will be easy for her to trust you or do you think she might be filled with fear? What might you want or need in these circumstances?

A woman who was chronically abused by her father for 15 years thinks about herself, her life, and her relationships through the grid of the abuse. She may have encountered situations where people proved trustworthy, but she does not trust. She may have heard thousands of words about how God loves her, but she believes she is trash, somehow an exception to the rule. Her abuse supports her strong need for control as a means of surviving the trauma.

This woman was a malleable child who absorbed lessons and beliefs about life, God, relationships, and herself in the context of ongoing sexual abuse. Children think concretely. They learn through their five senses. Her senses were continually assaulted while she was being treated like trash and probably told the same thing. Her beliefs will not be undone simply by words...words are how we do therapy, and yet words will not be sufficient.

She desperately needs someone who will keep on loving, who will endure and prove trustworthy. Those qualities have to be brought down into flesh and blood actualities. Human relationships have been smashed beyond recognition in this life. Trust, hope, and love are foreign concepts. The character of God demonstrated in the flesh over time is what this woman will need as she begins to tell her story and face the lies that have ruled her life. The therapist becomes the representative of this God to the survivor. The work of the therapist is to teach in the seen that which is true in the unseen. She has previously learned about fathers, trust, love, and refuge from one who emulated the father of lies. The unseen has been lived out before her and she has learned her lessons well. The therapist's words, tone of voice, actions, body movements, responses to rage, fear, and failure all become ways that the survivor learns about herself, relationships, and God.

As we untangle her belief systems and confront the lies, the reputation of God Himself is at stake in the life of the therapist. We are called to represent Him well.

For further thought:

The work of trauma recovery is often painstakingly slow. Look less to outcomes and more at your tone, actions, and responses. Note how you represent God to this person.

"We are therefore Christ's ambassadors."

2 Corinthians 5:20

Translators for God

Recently I was in Brazil speaking at two conferences on sexual abuse. It was one of those experiences that is life altering. I will not look at the world, the church, myself or my faith in quite the same way ever again. I gleaned many things from my time there and was richly blessed by the people of Brazil.

I believe God often uses life experiences as parables for us. He did so when He was here in the flesh and He often continues to teach us in that fashion. He turned my experience with a translator into a parable for me. My first translator was a young Brazilian man. We were different genders, cultures, professions, and life histories. He was my way in to the culture and the people. I needed his heart, his mind, and his mouth. He needed mine. I could not reach the people without him. He could not reach the people with what I had to give without me. I came to the people of Brazil through my translator.

Being translated is grueling work—for both parties. I had to present my thoughts in fragments. Lessons were given bit by bit. Periodically we would encounter a word for which there was no Portuguese equivalent. I would then have to find a way to describe and explain so the concept could be grasped. One of those words was "flashback." No one had heard of such a thing. I struggled to find a way to explain what a flashback was like and finally used a definition one of my clients had come up with years ago. A flashback is like having a nightmare while you are awake. As soon as they heard the description my audience knew what I meant. Many of them had experienced abuse themselves and had lived with flashbacks, not understanding what they were or how to respond to them. I had helped them understand themselves. Or, as a former client used to say, "You have explained me to myself."

Is all of this not a taste of the incarnation? Christ came in flesh. It was His way in to the culture, the people, and our lives. It still is. He needs our hearts, our minds, and our mouths in order to reach the people. We need His in order to teach them truth. John 1 tells us that Jesus came "to explain the Father to us." He also came to explain us to ourselves. It is through Christ and His Word that we know who we are and why we act the way we do. He has put accurate names to our experience of life and our selves in this world.

The experience of being translated requires a great deal of trust. The translator must listen accurately and speak truly. He must know two languages. He must know how to communicate both the words and heart of the one he represents. The speaker must relinquish a measure of control, and trust that the translator will take what is presented and accurately deliver it so the speaker is not misrepresented. The reputation of the speaker is in the hands of the translator. The translator also profoundly impacts the relationship the speaker has with the individuals in the audience.

IN OUR LIVES FIRST | 103

Is this not something like our lives as Christians? Are we not the representatives, the translators of God in this world? We must listen accurately and speak truly to the world. We must know the language of heaven and the language of men. Our lives and mouths are to communicate the words of God and the heart of God to the world. We represent Him and He has entrusted us with His reputation in this world. Others know Him and experience Him through our lives and our words.

I heard some funny stories about translators who purposely misrepresented speakers who were offensive or did not speak truth. However, it would not be funny for a translator to take the truth from a speaker and falsely represent what was said because he did not like what he heard or it went against his preferences or biases. Do we not, however, often do that to God? He says things that ruffle feathers and make us squirm. We alter them, soften them or neglect them. We make His thoughts adapt to ours rather than bowing to His words in our own lives and then representing Him accurately.

I was keenly aware that I had put myself in the hands (mouth) of another. I longed for the translator to know me, to understand my topic, and to grasp my love for the people. I wanted my listeners to receive my compassion for those who have been abused. I wanted them to sense my love. I wanted them to hear my strong belief that there is hope for healing in Jesus Christ. I wanted them to hear the truth about abuse and its effects. I wanted them to get an accurate set of facts. Their lives and the lives of many others would be impacted by what the translator gave them. Is this not a glimmer into the heart of our God? He has given us His heart and His words. Does He not long for us as His "translators" to represent His truths and His heart well?

For further thought:

Spend a moment with this image of translator. Consider how you represent His heart.

"The Word became flesh and made his dwelling among us."

John 1:14

Brief Meditation 7

"At last a day came when the burden grew too heavy for me; and then it was as though the tamarind trees about the house were not tamarind, but olive, and under one of these trees our Lord Jesus knelt alone. And I knew that this was His burden, not mine. It was He who was asking me to share it with Him, not I who was asking Him to share it with me. After that there was only one thing to do; who that saw Him kneeling there could turn away and forget? Who could have done anything but go into the garden and kneel down beside Him under the olive trees?"

Amy Carmichael[25]

---

[25] Amy Carmichael, *Gold Cord: The Story of a Fellowship* (Fort Washington, PA: CLC Publications, 1999), p. 44. Used by permission; see References.

Brief Meditation 8

"We exist to be of service.... Not a day, not an hour, of our lives lies outside that law. Not one personal habit, nay, not one personal habit of our most solitary and secret times (for everything tells upon character which is our great implement for service) lies outside that law."

H. C. G. Moule[26]

---

[26] H. C. G. Moule, *Thoughts for the Sundays of the Year* (New York: Fleming H. Revell Company, 1898), p. 130.

Week 5

The Many Sides of Power

Power is a word that carries negative connotations for many of us. We often associate it with the idea of oppression. However, power simply means the ability to do or act. It means to have impact. It is, in fact, something all of us have to one degree or another. It is a dangerous thing to have power and carry it about in one's life unthinkingly, something I fear many of us do. When was the last time you thought about the power you hold and how you are exercising it?

Power is a universal trait. Ever watch a two-year-old manipulate mom and dad? Power, however, is not a fixed trait. An individual's power varies with the context. I have power over those who work for me. I have power over my clients. I do not have power on the floor of the Senate. I have power over my sons because I am their mother. However, because they are both over six feet tall, they have physical power over me.

The other side of power is vulnerability. As I am physically vulnerable to my sons, so they are emotionally vulnerable to me. To be vulnerable is to be susceptible to injury or attack.

The word comes from the Latin word "to wound." A child is vulnerable to an adult. A client is vulnerable to a counselor. A patient in a doctor's office is always vulnerable, as is a parishioner in a pastor's office.

Whenever power is used in a way that wounds the vulnerable—that exploits trust—abuse has occurred. The word abuse simply means to use wrongly. When a person in power uses another who has come for help for his or her own ends, abuse has taken place. God called Ezekiel to prophesy against the shepherds of Israel. He told him to say "Woe to you shepherds of Israel who only take care of yourselves! Should not shepherds take care of the flock?" (Ezek. 34:2). Further on he describes the shepherds this way: "You have ruled them harshly and brutally" (v. 4). He is talking about shepherds who have been called by God and yet have used their power to feed off the sheep.

Understanding power

Let us make some things very clear about power. First, we can hold tremendous power and not feel powerful. You can feel tired, needy, fragile, and even powerless, and still wield tremendous power. Anyone who has parented small children has had days when she or he felt helpless and ineffective. Such things do not remove our power; they do, however, make us more likely to use it destructively. The more needy, fragile, and broken we feel while in a position of power, the more dangerous we are, because we are far more likely to use the sheep under our care for our own ends.

There are also many different kinds of power. Physical power is the most obvious. The bigger and stronger have power over the smaller and weaker. Physical power can also be found in presence rather than in size. I am sure you have experienced people whose personalities and charisma made them fill up and even dominate a room, even though their physical size may not have been great.

Another kind of power is verbal. Many of us in the counseling profession have this kind of power. Words are the way we make our living. Words are used to challenge lies, sway emotion, confront, and comfort. Those who are articulate can dominate a relationship, a conversation, or a room. Words can be used to get others to do what we want.

A third kind of power is emotional. Spouses have that kind of power over each other. Both parents and children can wield that power. Counselors have emotional power over their clients.

Knowledge and skill yield another kind of power. If I know more or have greater skill, then I have power in those arenas.

Finally, there is power in position. A CEO has power. A doctor has power. The President has power. A pastor has power. A counselor has power.

When these kinds of power reside in one person, it is a phenomenal combination. Think about it. Take a strong physical presence, an articulate voice, emotional sway, and psychological and theological knowledge and put them all together in a room with someone in crisis, whose struggles and pain have rendered them somewhat inarticulate, who is theologically uncertain and whose history carries instances of victimization—you have a potential for the *abuse of power*. Words, knowledge, skill, and position can all be used in concert to move or convince another human being who is vulnerable. Sheep are used to feed egos, give a sense of adequacy, build reputations, and feed sexual appetites.

How easy it is for us to forget that *all* power is derivative. Any of us who exercise power in positions of leadership exercise delegated authority. Jesus said, "All authority in heaven and on earth has been given to me" (Matt. 28:18). Any power we have is to be used on God's behalf, never our own, for the fulfillment of His purposes in the service of others. Any power exercised outside of obedience to God is not neutral or harmless but utterly destructive. Any time we use power wrongly, we follow the enemy rather than our Savior, who while holding all power, perfected it in weakness.

For further thought:

Consider the various types of power you hold—physical, emotional, verbal, intellectual, and positional. Are you reflecting your Savior as you wield power?

"Whoever wants to become great among you must be your servant, and whoever wants to be first must be slave of all. For even the Son of Man did not come to be served but to serve, and to give his life as a ransom for many."

Mark 10:43-45

Character: Leading from the Inside Out

It has been interesting to read and listen to the furor over those in political circles who have been in the news for their inappropriate sexual behavior. The headlines have been full of names over recent years: Clinton, Edwards, Spitzer, Ensign, Strauss-Kahn, and more recently, Schwarzenegger and Weiner. Why do some men in leadership engage in these behaviors? What are the causes? Does it really matter what they do in private? Is it anyone's business as long as they are performing well on their jobs? Is there any actual relationship between private and public behavior? The question, debates, and analyses keep the media supplied.

Many have argued that there is a distinction between public and private character. They believe that what candidates do in private is basically irrelevant and all that matters is their public behavior. Of course that line is now a bit blurred due to current technologies, as what would have been done behind closed doors in previous years is now being "sexted" and becoming public and global at lightning speed. The discussion seems to have shifted somewhat as a result, and there are those wondering whether or not who people are in private might actually impact who they are in public.

It seems a bit striking to me that we actually think those with a small amount of power, who act impulsively and cannot seem to control themselves even in their own self-interest, would automatically become wise, thoughtful, and nonreactive when given greater power. Or we have believed that someone who treated those in his private world abusively, using people for his own gratification, would actually treat his increased realm of "underlings" with dignity and respect upon receiving greater power.

This is, of course, not just a problem in the political world, but also a problem in the ecclesiastical world. We read again and again of powerful clergy and church systems that either abuse those who are weaker or cover up such abuse "for the sake of the Church." It is also not simply a male problem, as female clergy, teachers, and leaders have abused their power as well. The dynamic is a human problem and a challenging one for both leaders and followers. Clearly leaders who behave in impulsive, abusive, and self-serving ways have significant issues with grandiosity, entitlement, adoration, and power. However, many followers continue selecting such leaders and/or covering for them in a codependent way. Others have been blinded by the gods of charisma, expertise, power, and promises.

What fruit do you produce?

Surely one of the essential elements of a good and godly character is that whether in public or in private, those with less power are treated with grace, protection, and dignity. Think of the teachings of our Lord, He who holds all power. He has said something very profound about the link between public and private lives: "As a man thinks in his heart so is he" (Proverbs 23:7, NIV 1984). Or this: "Every good tree bears good fruit" (Matthew 7:17). Jesus is saying that it is not just what we do in private that matters, though surely it does; rather, who we are where no human can see or hear determines our true self! He also says that if you want to know what kind of tree you have, look at its fruit. He does not differentiate the arenas in which you observe that fruit. If there is rotten fruit behind closed doors—on the computer or off the stage—then you have a bad tree. Our God ties the whole of man up together—both the private and public heart. Character is first determined in the heart even before it is exhibited in what we would call the private life. It should be noted that no aspect of life is hidden from the God on His throne; there is no private life in that sense.

The problem of complicity

The other side of a leadership problem is the followers. Leaders without integrity can only get elected if there are followers who vote for them. Leaders who do not maintain integrity hold their powerful positions only if their followers are complicit in maintaining them in those positions. Complicity literally means "folded up together; an accomplice." When followers protect systems or leaders who yield rotten fruit, in essence they become complicit in their doings. Electing, maintaining or protecting leaders who have no integrity is to collude with them in the belief that the fruit in a private life has no connection to fruit in public. As followers, we compound the problem with our unchallenged support.

God has called those in leadership to two factors that we ignore at our peril. The first is a godly character, which includes things like integrity, faithfulness, self-control, goodness, and kindness. We are not to merely appear to have such qualities; they are to be part of the very fabric of our being. The second is that he/she who would lead or hold power is to be a servant. A servant of the people or a servant of the sheep does what is best for the sheep, not what is best for himself. It is my prayer that more leaders of this kind will rise up in both civil society and the Church, and that we who follow will not settle for anything less.

For further thought:

Integrity means we are the same inside and out. Ask God to reveal to you those places where you are prone to place self-love over service to God.

"We are that really, both to God and man, which we are inwardly."

Matthew Henry[27]

---

[27] Matthew Henry, *Commentary on the Whole Bible*, vol. 3 (1706), excerpted, Christian Classics Ethereal Library, http://www.ccel.org/ccel/henry/mhc3.txt (accessed 21 May 2014), Proverbs 23:7.

Responding to Institutional Sin

The Christian world has been slow to recognize and speak about institutional sin. Perhaps that is the Western influence with its focus on individualism and independence. Institutions are often complicit in, and even condone, evil, while at the same time speaking out against it, denying its existence and justifying it when it is exposed. As counselors, we have seen this dynamic play out in family systems. When we work with families where there is domestic violence or sexual abuse, for example, we encounter systems that fight exposure and work hard to preserve the status quo regardless of the cost to the individuals within it. We also know that churches have sometimes colluded with these families, believing that preservation of the system, no matter the evil it contains, is the biblical way.

It is not a big step to understand, then, that larger systems can fight for self-preservation, even while rotting at the center. The Catholic Church has been in the headlines in recent years for preserving itself, protecting its pedophile priests, and thereby allowing hundreds of child victims to spend their lives struggling with the memories and aftereffects of sexual abuse. We have more recently heard about mission organizations and Christian schools that have behaved in a similar fashion, refusing to believe the children and investigate their reports. And of course, this is not just in "those" churches or "over there." These evils occur regularly in evangelical, Protestant churches in the United States as well.

It is ironic how institutions, ordained by God and set up to preserve, protect, defend, and nurture, can end up devouring people in an effort to maintain the larger structure. It is reminiscent of Israel, a nation chosen by God and given rules and teachings so as to preserve *not* simply the institution, but the people within it as well. Israel, as a system, sadly became like the families with which we have often worked. She stood as a nation; her people continued to follow some of the teachings with their sacrifices in the temple and, all the while, she was rotting at the core and destroying the very people she was meant to protect. God's response was to obliterate the institution and scatter the nation like seed. He does not preserve structure with no regard for content. He wants purity in the kingdom of the heart, not the appearance of it in the institution that has to lie to make it seem as if it is present. He would rather the structure be destroyed *so that* He might work in the hearts of broken people and bring about transformation from the inside out.

His ways truly are not ours! Think about it. Can you imagine a global church, a mission organization, a Christian school, a denomination or a local church finding rottenness and deception in its midst and repenting to the point that the loss of the institution was subservient to obedience to Jesus Christ? What if power and words and resources were all used in concert to bring truth, reconciliation, restitution, and healing for the victims and the constituents? It is not our way. We are afraid. What if we lose all our money? What if we have to close down? We were established for good cause and will lose our opportunities in this world. Our organizations are not the kingdom of God. That is not where we will find Him. He resides in the hearts of His people who are called to live in obedience to Him even if it means their structures and institutions fall down around them. We are inclined to obey the institution rather than our God. In doing so, we are disobedient to Him and are calling evil good.

Jesus spoke very clearly when He told us that His kingdom *is not* of this world. His kingdom is to be the place where His will is fulfilled. No so-called Christian organization is His kingdom unless all aspects of that institution are governed by His will. So often we have preserved our institutions by pointing to the portion that follows His way, hiding or excusing those places that look nothing like Him; or by using a small part of His Word to justify the evil we allow to continue unhindered and unexposed. The true kingdom of God looks like the King Himself in all His glory.

I pray that we, in this generation, will have the courage to speak the truth about ourselves and our own institutions when they hide sin and pretend righteousness. I pray that we will bow the knee in repentance when sin is exposed in our families, our churches, and our organizations. Such a response is the fabric of revival, something much needed in this land and this world.

For further thought:

Consider the power you wield with your clients, especially power to name institutional sin. Pray for courage to speak truth to power for the sake of the name of Jesus Christ.

"Neutrality helps the oppressor, never the victim. Silence encourages the tormentor, never the tormented."

Elie Weisel[28]

---

[28] Elie Weisel, Acceptance Speech for the Nobel Peace Prize 1986, excerpted, NobelPrize.org, http://www.nobelprize.org/nobel_prizes/peace/laureates/1986/wiesel-acceptance_en.html (accessed 21 May 2014), para. 8.

Self-Injury in the Body of Christ

Through my work with those who have experienced child-hood sexual abuse, I have come across an issue that has only recently been discussed publicly—self-injury. It is an area full of shame for those who struggle with it, and as a result, it has been kept well hidden.

In recent months, I have been confronted more than usual with terrible and painful situations in the body of Christ. I have seen Christians destroying other believers, Christians behaving unethically and immorally, Christians vying for power no matter whom they hurt, and Christians lying to and manipulating their own brethren. In thinking about, and praying for, some of these circumstances, it suddenly occurred to me that I am again facing a situation of self-injury. I am watching a corporate body attack and destroy itself. I am wit-nessing self-harm with its accompanying dissociation, denying and numbing, so that injury can take place without the immediate sense of pain.

In working with clients who use self-injury to achieve certain ends—trying to make a "bad" person good, finding some level of false peace or gaining some sense of being alive—I have seen clearly that a way marked "death" can never achieve life. I have felt repulsed by what people do to their bodies (*not* repulsed by the people, but by what they are doing). I have known women who stick pins in their breasts, who cut themselves so extensively that they are reduced to cutting old scar tissue, and who do things we could not put into print.

I have encountered enough that I have struggled with vicarious traumatization as a result—and am trying to find a way to carry the knowledge that someone I care about is deliberately injuring herself, without that knowledge injuring me. When I encounter such practices I know I am looking at pathology. I am working with a broken and sick life. Healthy people do not deliberately hurt themselves. In fact, healthy people move away from any unnecessary pain.

But to the body of Christ—those who do things that destroy the body of Christ are also broken and sick spiritually. It is spiritually pathological to injure the body to which you belong. Like my clients, however, such people often call what they are doing by a different name, and think they are helping a "bad" person be good and believe that they are helping to solve a problem, rather than being one. *However, it is never good to lie to or manipulate a fellow believer no matter what you say your goal is.* It is never good to abuse power no matter how helpful you say you are being. Wrongdoing is never the path to right ends. The way of death never leads to life.

My sense of grief over the body of Christ has grown exponentially in the last decade. Our Lord's grief must be immeasurable! His body is not following her head. She is doing what she deems right or what she wants for her own comfort to achieve her own ends. Such choices mean she is repeatedly injuring herself. A client who hurts herself faces a great deal of hard work if she is to learn a new way. She must undergo a change of heart, of attitudes, of thinking, and of choices. It is no easy task to learn how to love and respect what you have previously trashed and mutilated.

It is my prayer that we who work with those who self-injure—we who know the brokenness, pain and twisted thinking indicated by such choices—will learn from those we seek to help. Anyone who injures the body to which they are united is sick. The injury may be violent or relatively small, but to harm oneself *and* believe it is for good is to be very broken indeed. May we work compassionately with our clients, holding the truth out before them, and intervening when necessary so that they may learn to live at peace with their own bodies.

May we also, as members of the body of Christ, never choose to injure that sacred body, already so wounded for our sakes, and may we be bold in speaking the truth when such injuries do occur so that we do not, by our silence, become passive partners in the harm that is done. May we never be those who, by serving our own ends, inflict further wounds on the body of our precious Savior.

For further thought:

The counselor exercises great power over clients. We are most prone to injure with our words, especially with those who irritate or attack us. Ask the Lord to enable you to speak only healing words.

"Just as a body, though one, has many parts, but all its members form one body, so it is with Christ.... If one part suffers, every part suffers with it; if one part is honored, every part rejoices with it."

1 Corinthians 12:12, 26

Loving the Poor and Needy

I continue to be amazed at the life and depth of the Word of God—especially how it comes alive in new and challenging ways. I can spend years reading and studying particular passages, thinking I understand, when suddenly I read it again and a new light from a different direction shines on that familiar Word, and I am given an entirely new thought.

It happened again recently as I was reading in the book of Ezekiel. I came upon verse 49 of chapter 16 and screeched to a halt. Here is what it says:

"Behold, this was the guilt of your sister Sodom: she and her daughters had arrogance, abundant food and careless ease, but she did not help the poor and needy" (NASB).

How many of us have read and heard sermons teaching us that the sin of Sodom was only sexual? We have then distanced ourselves from the Sodomites as being unlike us or seen those who fall into sexual sin as somehow abhorrent and certainly worse than we are. According to this Scripture, we have been wrong.

The verse was written to Jerusalem, the people of God. In other words, it was written to the Church. God's holy chosen people were told that they had lived more corruptly than those they had arrogantly condemned. God, the great heart-searcher, exposes in His people those sins lurking underneath and breeding those evils for which Sodom was known.

He speaks first of pride, that which made angels into devils and paradise into hell. Pride flows from abundant food and gives to itself all things. The Israelites were puffed up with their own prosperity and had no feeling for the needs of others. They had a self-centered and secure carelessness of ease and did nothing to reach out and grasp the hand of the poor and needy.

As the meaning of the words soaked in, I found myself asking God, "Is this a description of your church in America today? Are we following after Sodom rather than after Christ?" Could we be described as having pride, abundance, and ease? And could it be said of us that we have not reached out to grasp the hands of the poor and needy?

We have many descriptions of women and girls in our communities and around the world who are poor and needy. "Look," says our God, "look at the troubles that overwhelm and drain the life of these females who have been made in My image. Let it break your heart as it breaks Mine." He says to us counselors and pastors and missionaries the world over: "I am calling you out of your own circles and circumstances into the circles and circumstances of others."

To truly follow Christ is to set forth on a journey of ever-expanding benevolence, from the narrow limits of familiar territory into the dark and unfamiliar world of the oppressed and suffering. Such a journey demands a versatility of human sympathy, a power to pass rapidly from the interests of one to the interests of another. Is this not what it means to love the world that God so loved?

The labor of God in this world is a labor of love. It does not result in pride, selfish prosperity or careless ease. Like Him who demonstrated for us what love in the flesh looks like, this love of God in us is to go to the broken and needy and give of its wealth and labor without complaint. He came down into the haunts of human misery, and rather than rule by power, He ruled by broken-hearted sympathy.

Like our Master then, the strength of the kingdom is to be in its capacity to bear the weight of the burdens of this world. To be filled with love is to become the servant of all, to repeat the life of the Divine Man and become heir to His burdens. To Him belongs burdens not His own. He labors for humanity; He suffers their afflictions and is wounded in their battles. He is heir to the sins and sorrows of this vast world.

It is increasingly the cry of my heart that God will call His church to follow Him as burden-bearers, as those who share in burdens not their own. I long to have His body known for its capacity to bear the weight of the burdens of violence, injustice, trafficking, abuse, and oppression, rather than for its pride, its wealth, and its careless ease.

If we are to be like Christ rather than like Sodom, we will have to deepen our knowledge of the love of God in our own hearts. Our fruits will not be abundant if our roots are not deep. The crushing burdens of this world cannot be borne by the people of God unless those people have learned the breadth and height and depth of the love of God for themselves.

May we search out His love that surpasses knowledge so that we are filled up with all the fullness of God. And then may that fullness pour out all over the dark places of this earth so that the body of Christ in this age will be known for her humility, loving generosity, and labor of love for the poor and needy.

For further thought:

Meditate today on God's love for you and for His church. Pray to be empowered to bear the burden of love for others.

"Man says, God has taken hold of my name, Father; He has borrowed the human name of Father in order that I may learn how loving He is. Nothing of the kind. God has lent you His name of Father that you may know how loving you ought to be."

G. C. Morgan[29]

---

[29] G. Campbell Morgan, "Secret and Revealed Things," excerpted, Christian.org, http://articles.ochristian.com/article14171.shtml (accessed 21 May 2014), paragraph 12.

Brief Meditation 9

"If you obey God His order may take you into a cesspool but you will never be hurt."

Oswald Chambers[30]

---

[30] Oswald Chambers, *Disciples Indeed* in *The Complete Works of Oswald Chambers* (Grand Rapids, MI: Discovery House Publishers, 2000), p. 411, "Workers for God." Used by permission; see References.

Brief Meditation 10

"Yet listen now,
Oh, listen with the wondering olive trees,
And the white moon that looked between the leaves,
And gentle earth that shuddered as she felt
Great drops of blood. All torturing questions find
Answer beneath those old grey olive trees.
There, only there, we can take heart to hope
For all lost lambs—aye, even for ravening wolves.
Oh, there are things done in the world today
Would root up faith, but for Gethsemane.

"For Calvary interprets human life:
No path of pain but there we meet our Lord;
And all the strain, the terror and the strife
Die down like waves before His peaceful word.
And nowhere but beside the awful Cross,
And where the olives grow along the hill,
Can we accept the unexplained, the loss,
The crushing agony, and hold us still."
Amy Carmichael[31]

---

[31] Amy Carmichael, *Rose from Brier* (Fort Washington, PA: CLC Publications, 2012), p. 192, "Calvary's Elucidation." Used by permission; see References.

Week 6

Thoughts about Genocide and Femicide

Rwanda brought me face to face with genocide. I put a wreath on a mass grave (a quarter million bodies) and stood in a museum that made human beings retch.

In that museum, I stood before a plaque defining genocide. To commit genocide means any or all of the following: to kill members of a group; cause bodily or mental harm to a group; deliberately inflict conditions calculated to bring about the complete or partial destruction of a group; or impose measures to prevent births and forcibly transfer children of a group to another group. Genocide is in essence the destruction of a people group.

For 40 years, I have read, studied and worked with victims on the topics of trauma, abuse, and violence. I have listened to victims of rape, sexual abuse, domestic violence, genital mutilation, and trafficking. In recent years, I have traveled to other countries and seen and heard stories of what is happening to women around the globe. As I stood in front of that plaque, my mind began racing about what I have learned, and I came to a stunning realization.

This world is destroying its females. If you combine sex-selective abortions, female infanticide, female genital mutilation, child brides, rape, sexual abuse, domestic violence, and trafficking for bonded labor or prostitution, then you have the ongoing destruction of a people group—genocide. In fact, we should call it *femicide* and acknowledge that it is perpetrated on a global scale (interested readers will be fascinated by the *266,000 Google hits* on this subject and the *80,000 Google hits* on its close cousin, feminicide).

Oh, all femicides do not lead to physical death, though many do, but they lead to the death of minds, hearts, and souls. Little girls never allowed to be born, or killed at birth simply because they are seen as less valuable. Little girls brutally mutilated as a misguided attempt to control or somehow bring a man more pleasure. Little girls married at 10 or 12 years old, far too young for childbearing, and relegated to illiteracy. Little girls often victims of incest; and women raped or battered, not even knowing it is wrong. In many parts of the world, that also means being infected with AIDS—a death sentence. Little girls working 12 and 15 hours a day in forced labor, starving, essentially slaves. Little girls transferred out of homes, villages, and families to strange lands, forced to serve as prostitutes until they, too, die of AIDS.

Is this not femicide—a gender-wide form of genocide? There were shirts and signs and leaflets all over Zambia speaking out against gender-based violence. I was grateful to see them. What I want to know is this: How is that different from genocide?

As you know, these are not just events in Africa or Asia or someplace else. They are in every country. You see the victims of these vile things in your offices. You are often in the trenches working with them and the debilitating effects of such evil. You know what a dead heart and mind and soul looks like. You have also had the great privilege of watching resurrections, probably mini-resurrections as such work is only done little by little. It is a good work and so often rewarding—for it is, as I often say, a front row seat to redemption.

It is crucial, however, that we not miss the forest for the trees, so caught up in the little by little that we fail to see the larger picture. Do not just look at the individual woman or girl in your office who has broken your heart. Look at the world. We are destroying females, and it goes without saying that such a thing cannot be allowed to happen without also destroying boys and men. Those who violate little girls in such ways, which includes men and women, are also being violated. You cannot rape or kill without raping or killing your own soul. Fathers and mothers who kill their own daughters, or mutilate them, or sell them, are also killing themselves in some way. Men who satiate themselves with pornography or prostitutes are destroying not only the women they use, but themselves as well. We are destroying ourselves, male and female, over how we treat the girls and women of this world.

Oh church of Jesus Christ, His Bride, His Lady, will you not rise up and "open your mouth for the mute, for the rights of all the unfortunate? Open your mouth, judge righteously, and defend the rights of the afflicted and needy" (Proverbs 31:8, 9 NASB).

What if God's Lady really came to understand the plight of females (and therefore males) in this world? He who left glory and then while here went outside the camp to rescue a dying world, a people who were destroying themselves, has called His Lady to follow. His response to the genocide of the human race—for sin was killing us all—was to come down, enter in, and take on in order to redeem and bring life. Would He not have His church do the same?

Work in the trenches, serve the afflicted and needy, do the little-by-little redemptive work of counseling. It is His work.

But also, please lift up your heads and see the world. As you look, you who understand the soul damage of such things as abuse, speak to the Lady of our Lord and call her to loving action. May she not follow the world and turn a blind eye to genocide of any kind.

May she—may you, dear Christian colleague—instead face its horrors, its scope, and its evil. May the Lady of our Lord gird herself for action and enter into the fray for the sake of her Lord and Master, who did so for her.

For further thought:

Meditate on how God is calling you to fulfill His plan as expressed in the verses below.

"Defend the weak and the fatherless; uphold the cause of the poor and the oppressed. Rescue the weak and the needy; deliver them from the hand of the wicked."

Psalm 82:2-4

The Hidden Habits of the Heart

Some years ago I spent about 10 days in Burma (Myanmar), a country that had been in the news almost daily since the cyclone devastated a large portion of the nation. Of course the real cyclone in Burma was not the natural disaster, as tragic as that was, but the "cyclone" of corrupt national leadership—a brutal, utterly self-absorbed and tyrannical military regime.

The world was horrified to see leaders block outside assistance and risk the deaths of millions of people. The regime was willing to allow their people to die from starvation, typhus, malaria, and cholera rather than permit the entrance of those they call "foreign devils." Those who would bring relief, safety, and assistance were believed to be the destroyers. However, the real destroyers are within and the leadership's so-called "protection" will lead to the death of thousands.

My experience there was staggering. I have worked with abused people for decades, including abusive families and communities and churches. Burma was the first time I have entered into, and witnessed, an entire nation that has been abused. The generals at the top use oppression, brutality, force, intimidation, unpredictability, and isolation to control the people.

Tragically, such fear-based (as opposed to freedom-based) rule works. As one Burmese gentleman said to me, "The higher up you go, the more lawless it gets." No independent or creative thought is allowed. When a second political party was traveling through the country, those in power sent soldiers out to ambush them, beat them with iron bars, and then closed the hospitals so no treatment was available. Is it really any surprise that such "leadership" as this would bar outside help or allow thousands of vulnerable and needy people to die?

In reflecting on this and listening to people express anger, sadness, and shock at what was happening, I have been thinking about how awful things sometimes happen quite logically as the outcome of habituated behaviors. The terrible neglect of the generals of Burma was the logical outcome of decades of negligence.

Habituating to evil

My reflections have led to some sobering thoughts. It matters greatly what we continually practice and habituate. We become good at what we practice and if we practice it long enough, the behavior becomes automatic, easy, and natural.

Sadly, so can the justifications. We can practice an attitude or choice internally for a period of time with the result that a seemingly strange or out-of-character behavior occurs quite naturally—as if it were meant to be so.

For example, we can practice hatred and racism and emulate objectifying or demeaning thoughts until one day the decision to act on them comes so easily we do not even realize we have gone over a new line. The immoral and amoral become right and proper. The internal check of our conscience or the guilty flush in our faces no longer signals its warning bell.

Be forewarned, then, those of you who use and enjoy pornography. You cannot objectify others through the use of pornography for years and not have its morally corrosive effects eventually leak out into relationships with live people, even your own spouses and children.

You cannot nurse thoughts of leaving a marriage for months or years and not have that result in some form of actual leaving—either emotional or literal. You cannot fantasize an affair with a forbidden other and say "no" when the offer is surprisingly put before you.

The habits of our hearts and minds do matter. They shape us over time. As we nurture such internal habits, we are choosing again and again to bend our will to them until eventually the day comes when we can no longer choose a different course. We have become a slave to sin. And, like any slave, we automatically obey its dark demands.

I have studied the Nazi holocaust, the Rwandan genocide, and the Burmese tyranny. I have studied and sat with child abuse, rape, and domestic violence. Such things, national and individual, occur because over the years both individual and corporate will have been bent again and again, an attitude nursed, thoughts allowed, and choices engaged.

The small choices matter. The hidden habits of the heart matter. If we practice long enough, the unthinkable becomes doable, and the logical choice and devastation of our inner cyclones can be massive. We end up destroying ourselves, our families, our institutions, and even our countries.

No wonder that our God, whose habits are holy, tells us that He desires truth in the hidden places.

For further thought:

Our sin should never surprise us since it always springs from hidden habits of the heart. Ask God to reveal those subtle habits and to enable you to say no to them.

"Let us throw off everything that hinders and the sin that so easily entangles....fixing our eyes on Jesus."

Hebrews 12:1-2

Can the Church Rise Up in Ethical Leadership?

thical behavior: actions conforming to moral standards. The Bible reveals it like this: "Pure and undefiled religion in the sight of God our Father is this: to visit orphans and widows in their distress and to keep oneself unstained by the world" (James 1:27 NASB) and "to the extent that you did it to one of these brothers of Mine, even the least of them, you did it to Me" (Matthew 25:40 NASB).

Sometime ago I read a profoundly disturbing book by Victor Malarek, *The Natashas: Inside the New Global Sex Trade.* The sex trade is a global, twelve-billion-dollar-a-year industry. On the world's black market, human flesh is one of the top three commodities. This book tells the story of the thousands of women and girls from all over Eastern Europe who are sold for sex by networks of organized crime. They are lured with the promise of jobs and then sold into prostitution as human

chattel in an epidemic of modern slavery. Nations, governments, and institutions are turning a blind eye while every day
hundreds of thousands of women and girls are being raped in
brothels around the world. Surely, the earth is corrupt in the
sight of God and filled with violence (Genesis 6:11).

Malarek says, "The issue of trafficking desperately cries out
for firm, committed leadership; it has to be made a global concern." He and others state that it is the human rights issue of
the 21st century. Seeing it firsthand in Myanmar and South-
east Asia this past year, I would agree. However, when you
look at the record you see darkness and corruption everywhere—money, power, and politics speak louder than the
crushed lives of thousands of women. Governments have not
answered the call. And though there are many organizations
working tirelessly in this area, Malarek is correct when he says
it must be made a global concern. The scope of the problem is
so vast that a worldwide response is necessary.

What about the Church? She is global and she has a long
history of confronting plagues and freeing captives. It is clear
from the verses quoted above that God has called her to serve
as a humanitarian force in this world for those who are without help and resources. If Wilberforce and other Christians
could stop the African slave trade in the 18th and 19th centu-
ries, why can't we follow their example today? What if, in one
of the darkest hours on this planet, the global Church rose up
united and became known for her charity to those who are
being sold like chattel?

The Church exists in every country side by side with this
heinous crime. She who is called to live unstained by the
world can surely rise above the divisions of politics and culture in order to obey her Lord who came to set the captives

free. Why should she wait for or rely on governments to do her work? If the late Pope, John Paul II, had waited on his government in Poland for moral leadership, the world would look vastly different—be vastly darker—than it is today.

God has called the Church to diffuse her light. She is not to keep her privileges to herself, but to throw them over the wall, spread them abroad. Whatever she has she holds in trust for the world and what she has been given is to be used for the service of mankind to the glory of God. She is not to be swayed or silenced by money or power. She is not to fear the darkness, evil, and chaos. She is called to descend with Him into the lower parts of the earth, pass through dark places, and lie buried with the dead. She is called by her Savior to be like Him, seeking and saving the lost ones. Who could possibly be more lost, more dead, than a young girl sold into the sex slave trade?

What do you suppose would happen if the Church in every part of this world fell down on her face and pleaded with God on behalf of these women and girls? What if she began to seek out what He would have her do for these females? What if she became the global, committed, ethical, and moral leadership that is needed to fight this battle?

It is true she would have to crucify her pride, her love of comfort, and her selfishness. She would have to pause from her infightings and proliferation of book signings to sacrificially bend down to bring good news to the afflicted, bind up the brokenhearted, and proclaim freedom to the prisoners. But if she did, perhaps rather than the corruption and violence it now holds, the earth would be filled with the glory of God as the waters cover the sea (Habakkuk 2:14). And if she did, perhaps then the world would look and say, "They have been with Jesus, for like Him, they walk the way of those who are ready to perish."

For further thought:

It is easy to lose heart over the state of our world, to be paralyzed by hopelessness. But God is at work in big and small ways. Meditate on the evidences of God's sustaining power in your own life and in the lives you serve.

"On the back of the voice, which sets our hearts right with God, comes the voice to set the world right, and no man is godly who has not heard both."

George Adam Smith[32]

---

[32] George Adam, Smith, *The Book of Isaiah: Isaiah XL.-LXVI* (London: Hodder and Stoughton, 1890), vol. 2, p. 81.

Genocide Tempts Us All— Reflections on Rwanda

I have been to Rwanda.

I walked the streets of Kigali where bodies were stacked and rotting during the genocide in 1994. I've met with women who were deliberately infected with AIDS, talked with those whose heads were scarred by machetes, and heard from women who were prostitutes because, having lost their entire families at the age of 12 and needing food, they had no other recourse. The trauma of others' lives has been part of my life for 40 years now.

I have heard unimaginable stories, witnessed grief beyond measure, stood on Ground Zero when it was still hot, seen child prostitutes lining the streets of Brazil, and listened to the plight of the hideously oppressed Burmese. To paraphrase Bob Pierce, founder of World Vision, God has broken my heart with the things that break His.

It has been hard, but I am glad He has done so. He has given me a glimpse into His great heart for this sin-torn world. Truly He has been the treasure in the darkness.

One of the most sobering and grievous realizations of my readings and trip to Rwanda was my discovery of the complicity of the Church in the genocide. How can such a thing be? How is it that those who claim to follow the Crucified One can take up machetes against neighbors and friends or turn others over to those who carry them? How is it that a church that named the name of Jesus can now have an open Bible on its altar and be filled with the skeletons of those who died such hideous deaths in the place of hope for sanctuary?

It is frightening to think that those who say they are Christians can slaughter one known person after another in a very close, face-to-face way. Did they not know the Word of God would forbid such a thing? Surely they did. Did that not matter?

The answer is terribly complex. I do not pretend to be able to plumb its depths. I have pieces of knowledge that help me, but certainly not enough to truly explain such a thing. I know colonialism leaves countries weakened, without infrastructure and ripe for dictators and/or civil wars. We have seen that again and again. I know that grinding poverty and lack of education make people desperate and willing to follow almost anyone who says they can make it better. And I know something of the human heart. It is a heart "that is more deceitful that all else and is desperately sick" (Jeremiah 17:9 NASB). That means the heart is deceptive and tends to lead us astray from right precepts. But how does one's heart get *that* far astray?

Something fascinating came up in my study. One of the meanings of the word "deceitful" is "foot-tracked." As I searched, I found that this pertains to detectable evidence of a visible track of a substance. My husband and sons hunt. They know about detectable evidence of a visible track. They see it in the rubbings of buck in the woods. They see it in their footprints and in their droppings.

Basically, what that means is that if we look carefully, we will see that the deception of a heart over time leaves "droppings." It also means that we must go back to find the trail. The little steps of the trail, with its detectable evidence, will help us understand the outcome.

A heart does not become genocidal overnight. It does, however, leave evidence of its trail. Matthew 24:12 says, "Because lawlessness is increased [or, because iniquity abounds], most people's love will grow cold." Apparently there is no test of the heart that is as sure as when sin abounds. Genocide begins when I gain facility in doing a mean or heartless thing to a fellow human. Genocide begins when I malign my brother more easily today than yesterday. Genocide, rape, abuse, and the deliberate infecting with AIDS begin when I travel the crooked way more freely.

At the next level of darkness, when the poison ceases to sicken me, then my heart is desperately wicked. When the sting no longer wounds and the conscience ceases to upbraid, I have allowed iniquity to abound. Such things are the detectable evidence of a visible track of sin. They can result in genocide. Genocide is the systematic killing of a group of people. Do we see that when sin abounds in our hearts as individuals and as a corporate body that we end up killing ourselves and others? Murder becomes our common consummation.

As clinicians, we see the evidence of tracks in the lives of those who perpetrate sexual evils on children or of those clergy who feed on their sheep or those whose lives are controlled by a substance. These acts are not the slaughter of a people, but they do bring death to human beings. Such acts were not arrived at overnight. They came little by little. They move us inexorably from infanticide to suicide to genocide—murder exponential—darkness abounding in a straight line to hell.

Those of us who work with such deaths must be extremely careful not to catch the diseases that surround us. We must be careful not to assume that catching such diseases is hard to do. Working with sin, suffering, and evil can easily numb the heart. Numbness leads to death if left alone.

Listen to the voice of our Savior who calls us to "Come," lest we too become "foot-tracked." Come out of the cold that has numbed us, from the painlessness that deceives and the sin that no longer smarts. Come out to stand before the Light of the World, whose scorching Light will disturb us, but by whose stripes we will be healed.

May the "little" deaths never become comfortable and so lead us who name His precious name to bigger deaths. May we eagerly look for the God who searches hearts so that out of us will pour, not genocide, but rivers of living water.

For further thought:

Consider the following quote and ask God to protect you and to remain sensitive to the "sting" of sin.

"Sin takes from a man his healthy taste for what is good and his power to loathe evil, and then deludes him with the idea that he still has both."

George Adam Smith[33]

---

[33] George Adam Smith, *Four Psalms* (London: Hodder and Stoughton, 1896), p. 24.

Our Backwards Savior

The radical nature of Christianity is becoming more apparent to me as time goes by. It is my hope and prayer that this recognition is the work of God pressing my mind into the shape of the mind of Christ.

He has said that His thoughts and ours are not the same. It is amazing how, in spite of that teaching, we so often think God is like us in His opinions and positions. He keeps sounding pretty American and a very successful evangelical in His ways. Traveling to third world countries and dialoguing with their occupants has opened my eyes a bit more to who this God really is.

Frankly, He is quite different from anyone we have ever known.

So much of our culture is about achievement and success and the accumulation of material wealth. We are awed by mega-churches and we buy books that tell us how to succeed. We are hungry to be progressive, to get higher, have more, increase our numbers, and achieve yet another level.

Yet, the One whose name we bear often seems to be going in the opposite direction. In fact, He seems almost regressive. He goes back to gather up the lost things, those which have been left behind. He came to "seek and to save that which was lost" (Luke 19:10 NASB). His anointing was for the poor, the captive, the blind, the broken-hearted, and the bruised. The Messiah was anointed for weakness, slowness, disease, suffering, and death.

Jesus' work and words are not for strong souls. His message is for the weak. He, who lived in glory, regresses to earth. He, who was omnipotent, regresses to a human body. He goes back, He goes down, and He becomes small. By our standards of success, even those adopted by much of the American church, Jesus would surely be deemed a failure.

There are those who follow Him in His regressions. There are grandmothers raising grandchildren in our inner cities because the parents of those babies have died of AIDS. There are women walking alone into the barrios of the Dominican Republic to carry hope and life to those who get water only on Tuesdays and Saturdays. There are pastors in Brazil living in villages where all the men are alcoholics and batterers, and all the children are sexually abused. There are men and women in Burma who daily go into the projects where there is no clean water or sanitation to care for those dying of AIDS, and to teach skills to girls who are in danger of being trafficked.

There is a family in Swaziland who, at great sacrifice, cares for the disabled children who were thrown out on the trash heap because they were considered unfit to live. There are no wheelchairs, no medications, no safe restraints, and little food. These are people who follow the King who goes back.

What would it look like if the Church of Jesus Christ in the wealthiest country in the world followed Him backwards? What might happen to the ghettoes and deadly streets of our great and wealthy cities? What might be accomplished in the lives of our inner-city children who are not read to and often do not have sufficient books and supplies in their schools?

Globally, what might be done for the persecuted church that is filled with murdered brothers and tortured sisters with whom we will spend eternity? How might the Church around the world be strengthened and resourced to deal with the massive problem of trafficked women and girls from the very neighborhoods in which they worship? What could happen if we got down on our knees and asked God to teach us how to go backwards? To stoop down? To become small?

I do not know the answer to such questions in full, but I do know them in part. I know that barren parts of this dark world would begin to fill up with the glory of God. I know that joy would flit across the face of a suffering child. I know that the Church of Christ would look more like the bride of Christ and would function more like the soldier she is called to be.

I also know that you and I would be radically changed, for we would look more and more like the backwards and glorious Savior whose name we bear. We would be marked by love rather than success. We would be known as those who bend down, slow down, and reach down, just like the God who sits high and lifted up is now known for such things. We would be anointed to care for weakness, slowness, disease, suffering, and death. We would truly be enabled to "do justice, love mercy, and walk humbly with our God."

Does this sound like wishful thinking, a muse without a map? Is this merely a dream without a real hope? Not if we individually and collectively begin to ask God to make it happen. I believe He would answer such a prayer, because I believe we would be praying in line with His thoughts, instead of ours. Oh, may it be so. And may it start today.

For further thought:

Read Philippians 2:1-11, 13. Thank God that He will work in you for His good purposes.

"He delighteth to take up fallen bairns and to mend broken brows.
Binding up of wounds is His office (Isa. 61:1)."

Samuel Rutherford[34]

---

[34] Samuel Rutherford, *Letters of Samuel Rutherford: With a Sketch of His Life and Biographical Notices of His Correspondents* (Edinburgh: Oliphant, Anderson and Ferrier, 1891), Letter CVII, p. 220.

References

Quotations:

Unless otherwise indicated, Scripture taken from the Holy Bible, New International Version ®, NIV ® Copyright ©1973, 1978, 1984, 2011 by Biblica, Inc. ® Used by permission. All rights reserved worldwide.

Where indicated, Scripture taken from the New American Standard Bible. Copyright ©1960, 1962, 1963, 1968,1971, 1972, 1973, 1975, 1977, 1995 by the Lockman Foundation. Used by permission.

Carmichael, Amy. *Gold Cord: The Story of a Fellowship* © 1932 by The Dohnavur Fellowship. Used by permission of CLC Publications. May not be further reproduced. All rights reserved.

Carmichael, Amy. *Rose from Brier* © 1933 by The Dohnavur Fellowship. Used by permission of CLC Publications. May not be further reproduced. All rights reserved.

Chambers, Oswald. *The Complete Works of Oswald Chambers,* © 2000 by the Oswald Chambers Publications Assn., Ltd. Used by permission of Discovery House Publishers, Grand Rapids MI 49501. All rights reserved.

Meyer, Frederick Brotherton. *Christ in Isaiah* © 1995 by CLC Publications. Used by permission of CLC Publications. May not be further reproduced. All rights reserved.

Essays:

Day 1 - Counseling: A Dangerous Profession?
Previously published as "How's Your Immunity System?" in *Christian Counseling Today*, 2001, vol. 9, no. 4.

Day 2 - Finding Encouragement in Discouraging Work
Previously published in *Christian Counseling Today*, 2003, vol. 11, no. 4.

Day 3 - Prayer: The Crux of Our Calling
Previously published as "The Crux of Our Calling" in *Christian Counseling Today*, 2004, vol. 12, no. 3.

Day 4 - Boundaries and the Cause of Christ
Previously published in *Christian Counseling Today*, 2009, vol. 17, no. 3.

Day 5 - Eyes on the Master
Previously published in *Christian Counseling Today*, 2001, vol. 9, no. 1.

Day 8 - Obedience in the Seemingly Insignificant
Previously published as "Obedience, Sacrifice and Significance" in *Christian Counseling Today*, 2002, vol. 10, no. 4.

Day 9 - Vision: His or Mine?
Previously published in *Christian Counseling Today*, 2004, vol. 12, no. 2.

Day 10 - Entering In
Previously published as "Teach Me to Be Like You" in *Christian Counseling Today*, 2004, vol. 12, no. 1.

Day 11 - Are You Listening?
Previously published as "Only His Name" in *Christian Counseling Today*, 2002, vol. 10, no. 1.

Day 12 - In Our Lives First
Previously published in *Christian Counseling Today*, 2002, vol. 10, no. 2.

Day 15 - The Beginning of Deception
Previously published as "Some Thoughts on the Beginning of Deception" in *Christian Counseling Today*, 2008, vol. 16, no. 1.

Day 16 - Some Thoughts on Repentance
Previously published as "An Inward Look, Part 1" in *Christian Counseling Today*, 2001, vol. 9, no. 2.

Day 17 - Evidences of True and False Repentance
Previously published as "An Inward Look, Part 2" in *Christian Counseling Today*, 2001, vol. 9, no. 2.

Day 18 - Shepherding with Integrity
Previously published in *Christian Counseling Today*, 2000, vol. 8, no. 4.

Day 19 - Lured from Within
Previously published as "Seeing Our Inner and Outer Worlds Clearly" in *Christian Counseling Today*, 2006, vol. 14, no. 3.

Day 22 - The Crucible of Therapy
Previously published in *Christian Counseling Today*. Used with permission by Safe Harbor Christian Counseling, October/November 2009.
http://www.safeharbor1.com/html/Langberg-Crucible-Therapy-Article.php

Day 23 – Protecting Souls with Therapeutic Confrontation
Previously published in *Christian Counseling Today*, 2008, vol. 16, no. 4.

Day 24 - Resistance and Responsiveness
Previously published in *Christian Counseling Today*, 2007, vol. 15, no. 4.

Day 25 - Understanding the Trauma Survivor
Previously published in *Christian Counseling Today*, 2008, vol. 16, no. 3.

Day 26 - Translators for God
Previously published as "A Translation Parable" in *Christian Counseling Today*, 2003, vol. 11, no. 1.

Day 29 - The Many Sides of Power
Previously published in *Christian Counseling Today*, 2002, vol. 10, no. 3.

Day 30 - Character: Leading from the Inside Out
Previously published in *Christian Counseling Today*, 2010, vol. 18, no. 3.

Day 31 - Responding to Institutional Sin
Previously published as "Integrity from the Inside Out" in *Christian Counseling Today*, 2009, vol. 17, no. 2.

Day 32 - Self-Injury in the Body of Christ
Previously published in *Christian Counseling Today*, 2005, vol. 13, no. 1.

Day 33 - Loving the Poor and Needy
Previously published as "Women: A Labor of Love" in *Christian Counseling Today*, 2005, vol. 13, no. 3.

Day 36 - Thoughts about Genocide and Femicide
Previously published in *Christian Counseling Today*, 2007, vol. 15, no. 2.

Day 37 - The Hidden Habits of the Heart
Previously published as "Ideas Really Do Have Consequences" in *Christian Counseling Today*, 2008, vol. 16, no. 2.

Day 38 - Can the Church Rise Up in Ethical Leadership?
Previously published in *Christian Counseling Today*, 2004, vol. 12, no. 4.

Day 39 - Genocide Tempts Us All—Reflections on Rwanda
Previously published in *Christian Counseling Today*, 2007, vol. 15, no. 1.

Day 40 - Our Backwards Savior
Previously published as "His Thoughts vs. Ours" in *Christian Counseling Today*, 2005, vol. 13, no. 2.

About the Author

Dr. Langberg is a practicing psychologist whose clinical expertise includes 40 years of working with trauma survivors and clergy. She is the director of Diane Langberg, Ph.D. & Associates, a group practice in suburban Philadelphia, Pennsylvania, and speaks internationally on topics related to women, trauma, ministry, and the Christian life. Dr. Langberg is a clinical faculty member of Biblical Seminary and is core faculty with Biblical Seminary's Global Trauma Recovery Institute. She is the author of *Counsel for Pastors' Wives* (Zondervan), *Counseling Survivors of Sexual Abuse* (Xulon Press), and *On the Threshold of Hope: Opening the Door to Healing for Survivors of*

Sexual Abuse (Tyndale House), and is a columnist for *Christian Counseling Today.*

Dr. Langberg is Chair of the Executive Board of the *American Association of Christian Counselors,* serves on the boards of *GRACE* (Godly Response to Abuse in a Christian Environment) and the *Society for Christian Psychology.* She is also founder of *The Place of Refuge,* an inner city, non-profit trauma and training center. Dr. Langberg is the recipient of the *Distinguished Alumna for Professional Achievement Award from Taylor University, the American Association of Christian Counselor's Caregiver Award,* and the *Philadelphia Council of Clergy's Christian Service Award.* She is married and has two sons.

Made in United States
North Haven, CT
26 April 2024

51811713R00107